The Library of Pastoral Care

TITLES ALREADY PUBLISHED

**Sick Call: A Book on the Pastoral
Care of the Physically Ill**
Kenneth Child

Caring for the Elderly
H. P. Steer

The Pastoral Care of the Dying
Norman Autton

The Pastoral Care of the Bereaved
Norman Autton

Casework and Pastoral Care
Jean Heywood

Marriage Preparation
Martin Parsons

Principles of Pastoral Counselling
R. S. Lee

Pastoral Care in Hospitals
Norman Autton

IN PREPARATION

Marriage Counselling
Kenneth Preston

The Pastoral Care of Adolescents
Michael Hare Duke

Retreats
W. R. Derry (editor)

**In his own Parish
The Priest as Pastor, Prophet, and Servant**
Kenneth Child

Other volumes are planned

Library of Pastoral Care

PASTORAL CARE IN HOSPITALS

BY THE SAME AUTHOR

The Pastoral Care of the Mentally Ill
The Pastoral Care of the Dying
The Pastoral Care of the Bereaved

Pastoral Care in Hospitals

NORMAN AUTTON

Director of Training
Church Assembly Hospital Chaplaincies Council

LONDON

S·P·C·K

1968

First published in 1968
by S.P.C.K.
Holy Trinity Church
Marylebone Road
London N.W.1

Made and printed in Great Britain by
William Clowes and Sons, Limited
London and Beccles

SBN 281 02275 5

Contents

Acknowledgements

Thanks are due to the following for permission to quote from copyright sources:

Church Information Office: *Clergy–Doctor Co-operation: A Report.*

Constable & Co. Ltd: *The True Wilderness*, by H. A. Williams.

Epworth Press: *Christianity and Nursing To-day*, by M. Wilson.

Faith Press Ltd.: *Thoughts from the Notebook of a Priest-Religious*, edited by W. F. Adams, *S.S.J.E.*

Hodder and Stoughton Ltd and Harper and Row, Inc.: *Spiritual Therapy*, by R. H. Young and A. L. Meilburg.

National Association for Mental Health: *The Role of Religion in Mental Heatlh.*

Preface

The first book to be published in the Library of Pastoral Care, *Sick Call* by Kenneth Child, was written to help the parish priest in his ministry to the sick in parish and hospital. This present volume serves to complement rather than overlap it, for its primary intention is to assist the priest who serves as an officially appointed hospital chaplain, either in a whole-time or a part-time capacity.

Many chaplains will already be familiar with much of what has been written here, but some will be "beginners" in the field, and others might be considering undertaking such a ministry in the future. It is for these that this practical handbook has been compiled.

It is to be hoped that it might also be read by those who wish to understand more of the pastoral care of the sick in hospitals, and perhaps by members of the hospital staff themselves, who may desire to learn of the role of the chaplain.

I am grateful to A.C.C.M. for permission to quote extracts from a previous publication, *The Hospital Ministry*, Church's Ministry No. 6, 1966. My appreciation is also extended to the Bishop of Lichfield, Chairman of the Hospital Chaplaincies Council of the Church Assembly, for reading through the original manuscript and offering valuable suggestions, and to Mrs Jean Henderson, B.Sc., my secretary, for so carefully preparing the manuscript for publication.

Michael, my son, most kindly drew the various illustrations and Mary, his sister, helped in the compilation of the Index.

Whitsuntide   NORMAN AUTTON
1968

1

The Chaplain and his Ministry

More and more people are now becoming aware of the various professions at work within hospitals, yet it is sad that so few seem to understand fully the function of the chaplain in such a setting. It is doubly sad, of course, if the chaplain himself is uncertain or vague. It is therefore important that he should know *why* he is there. He will need to ask himself some basic questions as he undertakes his ministry. What does his chaplaincy involve and what does it mean, not only to staff and patients, but to himself? Is he there to counteract the "physical" with the "spiritual"? As the surgeon specializes in surgery does he specialize in sick-visiting? Does he come to dispense "religion" in the same way as the psychiatrist uses his psychiatry and the psychologist applies his psychology? While the doctor tends the body does he minister to the soul? In what way is his ministry unique?

This is the challenge of his chaplaincy, and herein lie its opportunities. The conception of his work in hospital must be clear and well defined in his own mind, for unless he himself knows what he is about he has little right to expect others to understand his position and so appreciate his presence amongst them. His role as chaplain must be as meaningful as medicine itself. His position must not be less professional than that of other members of staff, and his science and skill not less marked than those of the surgeon.

THE FUNCTION OF THE CHAPLAIN

Involving himself in his people's predicament he is to show them the Christ *already at work* in their midst. By the very fact of his priesthood he is called and set apart by God. In one sense therefore he is separated and unique. Yet he is also involved in a ministry which is truly incarnational, bearing the unbearable, sharing the unsharable, and entering into the heart of shattering pain with something more shattering still. He must be a man of prayer, for unless he prays his presence will have little significance at the bedside. His ministry can only transcend the immediate if he comes to his people from his altar or his prie-dieu.

He is there to give meaning to the very existence of the hospital and the purpose of the lives of those who share its work, attempting to make God more real and more relevant. He is there to be responsible for the spiritual life of the whole community so that each member, by his special vocation and ministry, may do all to the glory of God. He is there to interpret what God is all about, and to show what he is doing in and for those who are sick members of his Body. In binding up the brokenness of human existence he will endeavour to reconcile the patient to himself, to his neighbour, and to his God. It is true that many of his spiritual ministrations can be done equally well by instructed members of the staff or of the community, but his priestly function only he himself can perform; the eucharistic sacrifice only he can offer.

He comes therefore with no stethoscope or scalpel, but with instruments equally sensitive; with no drugs or doses but with remedies equally effective. He is chaplain rather than clinician and he works not to compete but to complement, not to supplant but to support. He it is who will be continually pointing away from the ordinary everyday activities to the extraordinary Source from whom they originate, linking human needs to divine resources, placing the natural in the context of the supernatural, and explaining the temporal in terms of the eternal. Often he will have to watch while others work; talk while others tend, listen, while others labour, and pray while others perform, but all the while his ministry will be one of Christian presence. He will be there and *there to stay*, for (as Erastus Evans has written):

When the psychiatric treatment has failed and the patient has committed suicide, the Pastor is there among the relatives facing insoluble problems, trying to turn bitterness towards God and life into softness and compassion for the human lot. He sits down beside the incurable to whom science can offer no alleviation or hope and whom medical treatment has to pass by, as beside one infinitely precious to God. He talks to the mentally sick although what he says does not seem to penetrate into his lonely and crazed world. He prays beside the dying who lies in a coma and has already cast off the moorings of this world. If the Pastor proclaims a hope that is not of this life, he must often stand silent before the hopelessness of this world. He must often feel as ineffective as the disciples watching the crucified Saviour, powerless to remove him from the Cross. But still he stays. It is his vocation to stand by crucified humanity; he stays as he would at the foot of the Cross. . . . There is meaning in the Pastor's presence, even though, from the scientific standpoint, he may have been regarded as useless.[1]

THE WHOLE-TIME HOSPITAL MINISTRY AND THE PARISH MINISTRY

To a young priest who feels a vocation to whole-time hospital chaplaincy it is important that he first be aware of the differences between a chaplaincy ministry and a parochial ministry. Fundamentally of course the work is identical, with its concern for people and their needs; the same shepherding and the same caring. There will be the inevitable limitations of time which both will suffer, but there will also be obvious differences:

1. In the hospital situation there often will be a deeper person-to-person encounter with its inevitable emotional and physical strain. The chaplain will be meeting new people every day, many of whom will be facing crisis situations, and the majority of whom will be in the throes of strain and stress.

[1] Erastus Evans, *Pastoral Care in a Changing World* (Epworth Press, 1961) p. 93.

2. Unlike his colleague in the parish, the chaplain will do most of his visiting before the public eye. He will play his part before a captive audience.

3. The parish priest is a *leader* of a community; the chaplain a *member* of a team—an essential member but *not* the captain.

4. The chaplain embraces the two worlds of theology and science, and consequently the language of his community will be to a certain extent different from that of the parish.

5. The parish priest will be ministering to people he knows; the chaplain to many whom he has never seen before and is not likely to see again. Of their various backgrounds he will have little or no knowledge.

6. The time factor in hospital will create difficulties in the exercise of his pastoral care. The frequent "turnover" of patients, the many interruptions, the visiting hours, the rest periods, the sedations, and the drugs will all tend to make a close relationship rather fragmented.

Such features only tend to make the need more imperative for the whole-time chaplain to create good working relationships between the hospital and the community. He can so easily become enveloped in the intricacies of hospital life that he loses touch with the Church at large. His ministry as a whole-time chaplain must be rooted and grounded in the work of the local parish and its congregation. If he walks alone he will soon become lost; he will remain isolated rather than integrated. The whole-time chaplaincy ministry, like all extra-parochial ministries, must be seen as a supplement to rather than a substitute for the parochial ministry. The chaplain will soon find that he needs more than "skills" and "techniques"—he needs a parish to support him. His hospital ministry must always be "patient-priest-parish" centred.

THE GENERAL AND PSYCHIATRIC
HOSPITAL CHAPLAINCY

There will of course be differences of approach in the psychiatric hospital. It is important that these be clearly outlined. Although many of the large general hospitals now have psychiatric units and the new district general hospitals will incorporate psychiatric services, the large psychiatric hospitals will be with us for some time yet. Apart from the obvious differences of size and the number of patients involved there will be others which are worth bearing in mind:

1. In many ways the psychiatric hospital chaplain will be able to fulfil a deeper relationship with his people than his counterpart in the general hospital, for although their numbers are multiplied the patients remain for longer periods. The normal stay of the patient in the general hospital is ten days; in the psychiatric hospital it is six weeks.

2. If his hospital is worked along the lines of a therapeutic community the psychiatric hospital chaplain can more easily be accepted as a member of the healing team. He will take his place in group discussions and ward conferences, and there will be more time for mutual consultation about the concerns of the patients.

3. There will be less of a group ministry in the general hospital and more individual work.

4. The general hospital chaplain will be involved in a more emergency type of ministry. The mysteries of life and death will be more marked. He will frequently be called to emergency baptisms and he will be continually administering the sacraments on the wards. In the psychiatric hospital the majority of the patients will be up and about and able to attend the services in the hospital chapel.

5. Interruptions will not usually occur as frequently on the wards and in the departments of the psychiatric hospital.

6. The psychiatric hospital is far more of a community. Many members of staff and their families live in the hospital grounds, and social life is far more prominent.

7. The chaplain will often find that psychiatric patients are more ready to discuss their fears and hopes than those who are in the general hospital. Their defences will be less great and they themselves less inhibited.

8. If he ministers in a psychiatric hospital the chaplain will need to have a thorough understanding of the more common mental disorders, the treatment given and its effect on the patient. He should also have knowledge of group work and counselling if he is to take his rightful place in the team and contribute to the treatment programme of the hospital.

PASTORAL COUNSELLING

In whatever capacity he will be serving as a chaplain, a great deal of his time will be devoted to counselling. With time on his hands the average patient has opportunity to think about some of his difficulties and tensions. Lying horizontally he often begins to think vertically. The principles of pastoral counselling will of course be similar to that carried on in the parish, but there will be certain important differences in the hospital situation of which the chaplain should take note.

1. The period spent in hospital will usually be a short one for the patient, so there will be little opportunity for any counselling in depth. It will therefore be necessary for the chaplain to refer the patient to the parish priest or minister, to the social workers, or to one of the social agencies in the community.

2. Because of circumstances, the chaplain will have to appraise the situation clearly and decisively. His approach will be more direct than in normal counselling situations, and he will often have to sift the important from the unimportant. He will be prompted to say, "We shall leave this for the time being; what matters now is . . ."

3. He must have a clear conception and understanding of the physical and mental condition of the patient to be counselled, for on no account must he tire his patient or lead him to become over-involved in a situation which will prove too burdensome or strainful.

4. He will often have to take the initiative, for the patient has not always chosen to consult the chaplain in the same way as the parishioner would ask to see his vicar; but he will avoid any appearance of inquisitiveness or curiosity.

5. The physical state of the patient may prompt his need to talk, yet his pain and discomfort can prove distracting during the visit to his bedside. The session will therefore have to be brief and to the point.

6. Many interruptions will occur in the general hospital situation, and conditions will be far different from the peace and quiet of the study at the vicarage. The chaplain will accept the majority of these as inevitable and deal charitably with the situation. In no way must he hinder medical or nursing procedures.

7. In hospital, team work is essential for the total care of the patient. Confidences must not be broken, but good communications between chaplain and consultant, sister, social worker are imperative. The chaplain must be prepared to work alongside the team in all his counselling ministry.

The differences between pastoral counselling and spiritual direction will be the greater attitude of permissiveness in the former. The relationship between the chaplain and the patient in counselling will end when problems have been resolved and he is able to act freely and independently. Spiritual direction will continue throughout the patient's life as greater spiritual growth is nurtured and developed.

THE ART OF PASTORAL CONVERSATION

The chaplain's most effective instrument is that of human speech. His speech at the bedside should never be a monologue. It will only make sense to the patient where it awakens a response. No conversation should be seen in isolation for, even though it may take place behind screens at the bedside and be of the most confidential nature, symbolically it is always within the context of the whole Church and Christian community. Studying as he must the art of pastoral conversation the chaplain must always bear in mind that feelings matter more than words. He will need to discover not only the meaning and significance of the words uttered but also the feelings behind them. He will speak not *at* the patient nor *over* the patient but *alongside of* the patient, keeping within his frame of reference, feeling and thinking with him. He will avoid the tendency to achieve too much in a few short visits, for he must not hurry the sick patient. It will always be better to be two paces behind than three in front. The tone of voice is most important, for its very intonation will symbolize acceptance or rejection, hostility or boredom.

He must always be conscious of a Third Person in his meeting. This will mean that he will not be too tied and bound by interviewing techniques nor by any "expertise", for all human speech should move freely in the light of the Holy Spirit and he will meet with the patient deeply conscious of the presence of Another. It is this that will make his conversation truly pastoral and so save it from being trivial and superficial.

THE ART OF COMMUNICATION

The chaplain has to learn to interpret the good news of the gospel in terms each patient can understand. In one or two visits he has to attempt to say something meaningful, so he will speak not in clerical clichés but in terms of a contemporary Church. It is related of Father James in Graham Greene's *The Living Room* that every time he opens his mouth his "tongue is heavy with the . . . catechism". He may be so anxious to get across what he wants to say that in his very anxiety he will violate the principles of communication. Torrents of words can so easily block the relationship and act as a protection for his own insecurity:

> You say expected empty things
> You speak in pious tones
> You call on God to heal the man
> When
> What you really say is
> "Get me out of here".[1]

If there is open and free address between chaplain and patient as person to person, unfettered by any defences or undue anxieties, then the pastoral call becomes meaningful and the conversation a dialogue rather than a monologue. The encounter at the bedside then becomes "personal" and in this union of two personalities both are changed. True communication takes place when the chaplain sees the patient as a person, abandons his artificiality, and parts company with his prejudices. When he sees the patient he sees himself; when he ministers to the patient he ministers to himself. It is only then that true empathy can take place. The unspoken language of the patient "I need you" is met by a similar response from the chaplain "And I need you". It is this non-verbal communication which is all important to the chaplain, for true verbal communication can only be based on acceptance at the non-verbal level: the sigh, the groan, the tear, the grunt, the facial expression, should all speak to the chaplain. Real communication is no mechanical process, but rather a dynamic interaction between the chaplain and the patient. It is a two-way process far deeper than words, for so often in the sick-room words only

> Strain,
> Crack and sometimes break, under his burden,
> Under the tension slip, slide, perish,

[1] "Philadelphia General Hospital", by Daniel DeArment quoted in *The Journal of Pastoral Care*, Vol. XX, No. 2: June 1966, p. 95.

Decay with imprecision, will not stay in place,
Will not stay still.[1]

Communication is the total acceptance of the patient, his anger, his resentment and his hatred, as well as his hopes, his fears and his aspirations.

THE ART OF ASKING QUESTIONS

Some questioning will be necessary to establish relationships with the patient, but the chaplain will avoid at all costs any tendency to cross-examine. The patient on admission or immediately afterwards has already been asked innumerable questions and will not take kindly to the repetition of these, e.g. "Hello, Mrs Smith. How are you? When did you come in? How long have you been unwell? Do you live in the district?" His questions will therefore express his interest rather than satisfy his curiosity. He will avoid asking questions which only require "Yes" or "No" for an answer. It is preferable to ask "How are you feeling about having the operation tomorrow, Mr A?" rather than "Are you having the operation tomorrow, Mr A?" More emotional material will be available to the chaplain in this way, and he will be able to picture the patient as a "person" and not just another admission. Herein lies the art of questioning in the hospital situation, for (as it has already been made clear) it is the patient's feelings which are all-important.

Direct questions will not get the chaplain very far in his pastoral care, and if questions are not handled discreetly they can so easily disrupt the whole relationship. If he can slowly and gently feel his way into the patient's fears and anxieties, he can then approach without causing undue alarm or in any way seeming to attack the "person" of the patient. The conventional "Hello, Mr Smith, how are you?" is so often fruitlessly superficial. If Mr Smith replies "I'm fine, thank you" the chaplain has to start again along a different track, and the line of communications becomes blocked.

[1] T. S. Eliot, *Four Quartets* (Faber, 1959) pp. 149f.

The asking of too many questions will mean that the chaplain is so insecure and anxious that he wants to hold on firmly to the conversation and direct it into areas which will not prove too threatening for him. Such questioning puts the chaplain "in front of" rather than "along side of" the patient. With less questioning the conversation will have more depth and certainly more meaning.

THE ART OF LISTENING

As with our speaking, so too with our listening. To be effective it must be embedded in our own speaking and listening to God. "Many people", wrote Bonhoeffer, "are looking for an ear that will listen. They do not find it among Christians, because these Christians are talking where they should be listening. But he who can no longer listen to his brother no longer listens to God either: he will be doing nothing but prattle in the presence of God too." To listen is no passive, negative exercise, but is active and positive. It requires complete attention to every detail in the personal encounter. It will mean interpreting shades of meaning, the significance of gestures, and the implication of responses. The chaplain will not only listen therefore, but attempt to understand and discover the feelings behind the words expressed.

Listening is not merely keeping quiet while the patient talks. Rather is it a highly professional aptitude, for only he will hear who listens intelligently and competently. He will hear not only what is said but what has been left unsaid, being sensitive enough to discover unspoken needs and hidden anxieties. He will also hear not only the superficial but that which has been subtly suppressed. If the chaplain listens with his eyes as well as his ears he will soon discover that sick people communicate all kinds of attitudes and emotional reactions by their very gestures. If words are taken at their face value he will miss the underlying hostility which might be covered by a smile or the deep depression hidden behind bright chatter. So much of what is potentially being communicated will escape him. In his listening he may be verbally inactive, but unless he is mentally active he will not understand what the patient is trying to convey.

If his listening is biased patients will be bored. If it is impaired they will be inhibited, and if it is distant they will soon be discouraged. By developing the art of listening the chaplain will enable the patient to answer for himself so many of the questions he has raised, and to discover for himself so much he has sought. By such silent co-operation he will register such concern for his patients that they will be heard where they most need to be heard.

WHAT THE CHAPLAIN SHOULD KNOW

To be competent in his hospital ministry there are certain foundations on which that ministry must be built, namely:

Spirituality. Before he can be open to other people he must be committed to God. His own prayer life must be strong before he himself can offer prayer in the hospital chapel or at the bedside. His own sacramental life must have meaning to him before it can be made real to others. In his spirituality he will have to ponder over the relation of *holiness* to *wholeness*.

Theology. The chaplain, faced as he is with some of the most difficult and crucial situations in life, must have a sound theology on which all his pastoral care must be based. He will need a strong positive faith in *God as Creator*, the Maker. He will work out the significance of the new discoveries of science, surgical techniques, etc. in the light of his theology. He will see *God as Redeemer*, rescuing and liberating man and enabling him to be his true self. The fears that torment modern man, and the sins which obstruct his spiritual growth, can only be remedied by him who came to set men free that they might have life and that more abundantly. *God as Sanctifier* will help to emphasize the fact that unless the chaplain has an adequate theology of the Holy Spirit he will labour in vain. He must needs ask what has *theology* to give to *therapy* and what has *therapy* to say to *theology*.

Psychology. He must have an understanding of the tenets of normal and abnormal psychology, coupled with an ability to apply such understanding. He must be aware of his own limitations and potentialities, of his own strengths and weaknesses. Many of the moral problems with which he will have to deal will have psychological roots which he must attempt to explore. The study of human growth and development will form a most necessary background to his ministry and help him to serve his people with discretion and understanding. Unless he has this knowledge of psychology he will tend to become too authoritarian, too dogmatic and moralistic. He will fail to appreciate the deep underlying causes of behaviour and so be denied a very necessary part of his equipment in ministering to the sick. He will need to know himself, understand himself, accept himself, and be himself.[1] He must examine the interaction of *psychic conflict* and *physical disease*.

Sociology. If he is to function efficiently in the setting of a large hospital he must familiarize himself with the administrative structure of the hospital service within the National Health Service (see Appendix A) as well as the sociological factors involving hospitals and their communities. It will be essential for him to know of the work of the social agencies in his area and so cooperate with them and the hospital psychiatric/medical social worker. The patient must never be seen as an isolated individual but placed in the context of his environment, his home and family, etc. *Sickness* must be seen in the framework of *society*, for no real therapy can be fully worked out in individualistic terms. True healing can be seen only in the context of *total healing* of an individual who is part of society.

The patient. When the chaplain visits a ward of fifteen

[1] For further study see André Godin, S.J., *Psychology and Pastoral Care*, Chapter 1: "The Pastor as Counsellor" (Logos Books, Gill & Son, 1965).

patients all will appear very much the same, but to minister individually presents the chaplain with a variety of emotions, ideals, and aspirations. He will attempt to know as many patients as possible, but because of the limitation of time it is important that he spend more time with those who are in the greatest need.

The problem.   The chaplain must discover the main concerns of the patient and how best he can meet his needs. Some information about the patient will therefore be essential. If he wins the confidence of the hospital staff and if his relationships with the doctors and sisters are good, he will be kept informed of all relevant and important information. He should regularly be sent lists of newly-admitted patients, those who are undergoing surgery, and the dangerously ill and dying patients. If it is possible for him to be provided with a list of those patients to be discharged he can then more easily commend them to their parishes. It is essential that he be kept up to date with all information relating to his work.

The pain.   He will be sensitive to the hopes and fears of the patients, and it is important for him to know how to bear the pain and suffering of those he comes to tend. To feel what they feel is a very difficult exercise, but unless he becomes involved in their very predicament, their tensions and their anxieties, much of his work will remain only on the surface. If he is to help suffering people he must be prepared to suffer himself.

> Dear Lord and Father of mankind,
> Forgive our foolish ways . . .
> Let sense be dumb, let flesh retire . . .
> Speak . . . Speak . . . Speak
> Oh God, but how?
> Help me not to run away
> This time.
> Help me to feel, to share, to know
> Their pain and not my own.[1]

[1] "Philadelphia General Hospital", Daniel DeArment, ibid.

Entering the valley of the shadow with his patients, it is important for the chaplain not simply to *go down* hand in hand, but for both to *walk through* that same valley; then they will fear no evil, for God will be with them. Without this realization the chaplain will either be forced to adopt a cold objective approach, remaining aloof and uninvolved, or become so immersed that he will be totally unable to deal with such situations. Unless he is at all times conscious of his own insufficiency for such a ministry of self-oblation he will soon falter and fail. He will be adequate only when he accepts his own inadequacy.

WHAT THE CHAPLAIN SHOULD DO

Care. "Caring matters most" (von Hügel) and caring lies at the very heart of the healing ministry. The whole Christian community should share in the chaplain's caring, for pastoral care is the concern of the Church, both priest and laity. It will be the Christian community which will extend and give completion to the chaplain's ministry. In sharing it will be caring.

The Church as the Body of Christ is at work in and through the chaplain, for he is in the hospital not as an individual but as a representative of that Christian community and is always acting on behalf of the congregation. When the chaplain prays, with his prayers go the intercessions of his whole people, surrounding and supporting both the patient and himself. The whole congregation should therefore share in his work and care in his caring. It will then be fulfilling its vocation as a healing fellowship, the very Body of Christ.[1]

It is becoming more and more evident that the ministry of healing is moving outside the hospital[2] and so it is increasingly

[1] For the role of the congregation in Christian Healing, see J. Wilkinson, *On the Healing Church* (Tübingen Report, World Council of Churches, Geneva, 1965), and *Health: Medical–Theological Perspectives* (Tübingen Report, W. C. C. Geneva, 1967), pp. 35–61.

[2] *Vide* Kathleen Jones, *The Compassionate Society* (S.P.C.K. Seraph Book, 1966) p. 49.

urgent that the chaplain teach and train his congregation to become a redemptive fellowship. In this way much of the over-professionalism of the priest will be submerged into a doctor-clergy-congregation partnership.

Comfort. It will be part of the chaplain's work to strengthen the patient by his presence, his prayers, and the sacraments. Comforting will be a necessary stage in understanding the patient, but it will be no weak, insipid, sentimental approach, for, as somebody has written, "true pity is the strong gentle pity of the saints. . . . It is powerful and devouring, not snivelling and weak. It is one of the strongest passions of man." As he stands at the bedside he will attempt to instil faith for fear and hope for despair. He will encourage the patient to out-grow much of his dependency and introspection and so help in the recovery from illness to health.

Challenge. All sickness is a challenge for it can lead either to bitterness or to betterment. Our Lord always approached people with a loving and caring concern, but where necessary he challenged: for example, his conversations with the Samaritan woman at the well (John 4) and the rich young ruler (Mark 10.17–22). So much of suffering will appear wasteful and purposeless to many; cutting across the meaning of life itself, and frustrating their hopes and desires. It will tax courage and test faith. "It is rather like having to pass an examination", writes Olive Wyon (*The Grace of the Passion*, p. 32) "which is absolutely necessary if we are to do the work we want to do. There is no getting out of it. . . . In a sense Jesus himself had to pass this examination when he 'learned obedience by the things which he suffered'. He passed it at every stage, up to the last moment of his life." If the chaplain can help his patients to pass successfully some of the "examination papers" which are set and test their results by Christ's, then much of the torment of suffering will be transformed; a deeper meaning will be discovered and a greater peace gained.

Relate. Relationship has been called the soul of casework. Such an analogy is equally applicable to the chaplain's ministry. Without good relationships between himself and the others in the hospital community, much of his work will be thwarted and he himself frustrated. He may have the most pleasing bedside manner, say all the right things, and visit most prodigiously, but if his personality is such that he cannot relate with either patient or staff then the very essence of his chaplaincy will be missing. The chaplain cannot expect others to be free when he himself is reserved and inhibiting. If he is thus handicapped by such restrictions then he will meet serious difficulties throughout his hospital ministry. He must be open and receptive, easy and free (not "free and easy"!), with a sensitive understanding of and response to the fears and feelings of others. By his approach to his patients he will create an accepting atmosphere in which they will be free to discuss their problems, and a dynamic interaction is fostered between them.

Refer. Serving, as he must, as an intermediary between hospital and community, it will be an important part of the chaplain's function to commend patients to their respective parishes on discharge from hospital, and to refer many who are out of touch with organized religion, provided their permission has been obtained. This is particularly important in the psychiatric hospital, for unfortunately shame and stigma still exist in the minds of many and the "outside world" can be most threatening and unsympathetic. The chaplain will refer not only patients but also members of the staff who leave to serve another hospital or take on different employment. He will in turn be eager to receive commendations from priests and ministers about members of their congregations who are to be admitted to hospital as patients or to be employed by the hospital as staff. This is particularly important with regard to new student nurses, for it is no longer necessary for them to give their religious affiliations when they are interviewed and if the chaplain works in a large teaching hospital it becomes extremely difficult to get to know members of the nursing staff individually.

Not only must he refer to the outside community, but also to other professions within the hospital itself. During his ward visiting there will be occasions when he will refer some of the patients' difficulties to the medical or psychiatric social worker, or the lonely patient without visitors to the League of Friends. He must be alert to all possible channels for furthering good communications.

Respond.   In his verbal response to the sick patient the chaplain must always be genuine and sincere, for those who are ill soon sense any false aspect which is adopted to hide the real self. "The clergyman's unction", writes Hadfield, "the physician's professional manner at the sickbed, the lawyer's wise mien, the saleswoman's jaunty jargon, are all of them indications of signs of weakness resorted to in order to cover the poverty of the real self."

But genuine response need not necessarily be verbal. It is the unspoken response of internal *feeling* and *identification* which is all important. If the chaplain gives due attention to the internal feelings then the external expressions will usually show a sensitivity and warmth which are essential elements in any real relationship.

WHAT THE CHAPLAIN SHOULD HAVE

Confidence.   Good intentions are never enough in our dealings with sick people, for the chaplain cannot afford to falter or fail. He must approach with confidence, for if he himself is insecure or tense then he will inspire neither patient nor professional staff. By his very bearing he will bring poise and calm to those who are disturbed and strength to those who are weak. The young nurse and houseman will soon sense his confidence and be more ready to consult him; the patient will soon realize his worth and be more prepared to express his feelings, and the hospital will be aware of his contribution and include him in their consultations.

Although he may feel inferior and inadequate before so much competence and skill which a hospital environment presents, he will know that he brings something that others need if they are to leave hospital not only physically improved but also spiritually changed.

Compassion. The chaplain should be the outward expression of the compassionate love of Christ. "Inasmuch as ye have done it unto one of the least of these my brethren, ye have done it unto me" (Matt. 25.40). By his deep concern for and commitment to the patient he will become more and more responsive to the needs of the sick. He will be signifying the care and love of the whole Church by his friendly interest and his emotional understanding, endeavouring as far as is humanly possible to suffer alongside the patient in distress. "Compassion", writes H. A. Williams in *The True Wilderness*,

> means that when this or that person happens to cross our path we should be sensitive to understand the nature of their need and identify ourselves with them in this predicament, getting inside their skin. . . . This identification of myself with another person, in so far as it is real, is a costly business. . . . It is in the realization that he and I are in the same hell, that true compassion is born and grows. It is not that I am healthy and he is diseased. We both suffer from the same wounds, and that is how we can meet and communicate with each other. . . . . "There but for the grace of God go I" sounds pious, but it speaks not of compassion but of superiority. Compassion says, "There, by the grace of God, I have been and I am" (pp. 99–102).

Courtesy. Good manners in hospital are essential. The chaplain cannot demand attention and co-operation, but he can win it by his whole manner and bearing. He will be discreet and tactful about the information he may gain about both patient and staff, and he should be an example "in word, in conversation, in charity, in spirit, in faith, in purity" (I Tim. 4.12). He should always remember whose he is and whom he

serves (Acts 27.23). The silent language of example will then
be made evident to the most senior consultant and to the most
junior nurse. It should be seen by his words, his behaviour, and
his whole manner that he is a servant of God, upholding the
dignity of his office as hospital chaplain.

Before he enters the ward the sister's permission should be
sought. When times of services either in the ward or in the
chapel are being arranged the matron and her staff should be
consulted. The common courtesies can easily be overlooked
when the chaplain endeavours to carry out his work within a
limited time-span and so has very little opportunity of con-
versing with various members of the hospital staff. When he
takes up his appointment as chaplain he should be prepared to
call on the various departmental heads and make himself
known to them,[1] and courtesy calls should be made from time
to time to the offices of both junior and senior members of the
staff. Whether he realizes it or not, knowledge will be taken of
him, and all around him should be able to see his very presence
in hospital as "an outward and visible sign of an inward and
spiritual grace"; a "pledge" whereby they are made aware of a
power behind them, and a "means" whereby they are drawn
and helped towards it.

Patience. Difficult as it often is, the chaplain will avoid all
signs of hurry and rush, and the tendency of seeing the maximum number of patients in the minimum amount of time. If
he flits from ward to ward in an endless round of visits he will
do little constructive work. Other people's work in hospital will
perhaps appear far more sudden and spectacular. The surgeon
in the theatre operates and the patient is home in a week; the
physician tries a new drug and the pain is immediately alle-
viated; but the chaplain, like the parish priest, often sees very
little visible sign of his ministry among his people. He will have
many disappointments and frustrations when few respond to
his ministry. People in hospital come and go in rapid succession. The majority of staff reside outside in the community,

[1] See *Notes for the Guidance of the Part-time Chaplain*, CIO, 1962.

and perhaps only a few attend the hospital chapel. But he will learn to "take no thought of the harvest, but only of proper sowing",[1] and so labour to bring forth fruit with patience.

Gentleness. Sick people are very sensitive, and faith must be found, not forced. The chaplain must never attempt too much in a short time. His visits will be frequent but they must also be brief. There will be no place for argument or harshness at the bedside but a true sense of humility, for often the chaplain will be not so much concerned to give patients what he has as to teach them how much they themselves have to give. Gentleness only springs from self-awareness and an acceptance of our true selves with our failings and shortcomings. As H. A. Williams writes,

> Then I am able to accept perversities and failures in other people because I know that I am in the same boat as they are and that my only hope, like theirs, is that God wills to have mercy upon all men. Then I can be of a gentle spirit, for I am finding my security not in what I am but in what God is. Such gentleness towards other people is the way in which Christ sends us into the world as the Father sent him. It is the most real and effective form of evangelism. . . . When a man feels that somebody accepts him, blemishes and all, without any sort of strings attached, then for that man the kingdom of God has drawn near with its power to heal and raise from the dead. For in all gentleness Christ is present, verily and indeed, and in his real presence is the power of God unto salvation.[2]

Love. The love of God can only be seen through human relationships, and the whole hospital should strive to be a loving community. This is doubly important for the psychiatric hospital chaplain for much conflict in the mind is caused by the lack of security and the fear of being unloved. "Love is

---

[1] T. S. Eliot, *The Rock.*
[2] "Gentleness": H. A. Williams, in *Theology,* September 1962, pp. 357–8, reprinted on pp. 8–12 of *Traditional Virtues Reassessed,* ed. A. R. Vidler (S.P.C.K. 1964).

the ground of our being" [1] and if the chaplain is to give himself to the uttermost in love then he must be prepared to accept everything he finds in the person of the patient or member of staff. Love will include respect for the worth of each individual and concern for his dignity. But is the chaplain ready to be so involved? Is he afraid of being deprived of his authoritative role and instead of being "a prophet who thunders from Mount Sinai" becoming "a suffering servant who bears the woes of others"?

WHAT THE CHAPLAIN SHOULD BE

Available. The more the chaplain is seen the more he will be known. It is therefore important that a room be put at his disposal in the hospital which is centrally situated and equipped with telephones. It is equally necessary for him to be included in whatever "call system" is used at the respective hopital, so that he may be found whenever needed. It is always helpful to inform the hospital switchboard of his time-table and parochial programme (if he is part-time) so that he can be contacted without unnecessary delays.

A chaplain should also be available *personally*, with an open receptivity which prompts others to come to him and share their difficulties and problems. Nurses must see him as one whom they can approach freely, doctors must recognize him as one to whom they can turn for advice and counsel at any time, and patients must sense that he is always receptive to their concerns and interests.

Acceptable. The Chaplain must be aware of what qualities or features he possesses which may jar or disturb his relationships with others. His own personal appearance must be watched; his poise and propriety noted; and any unpleasant mannerisms counteracted. His whole bearing should bring confidence and calm. He should always bear in mind that the patient is host

[1] See J. A. T. Robinson, *Honest to God* (S.C.M. Press, 1963) p. 46.

THE CHAPLAIN AND HIS MINISTRY

and he the guest. Dr Walter C. Alvarez tells of the patient who asked for another doctor because the one who attended her at the bedside had his collar torn half an inch at the side: "I thought if he was so careless in his dress he probably would be careless in other things." [1]

Adaptable. It will be part of the chaplain's work to "rejoice with those who rejoice and weep with those who weep". He will move from bedside to bedside and will have to adjust his mood to meet that of each individual patient. To move from the sorrows of patient A to the joys of patient B and not infect the one with the feelings of the other needs careful watching. He will minister to patients not only with different views of churchmanship but also of varying social and intellectual backgrounds. He is the chaplain to them all, and so must be quite flexible in his ministry to each of them.

It is important however that in his endeavour to be "all things to all men" he does not water down his own spiritual ministry so that it becomes too weak and insipid to be effective.

Sincere not suave. "Sincerity", Tournier tells us, "is the *sine qua non* of the dialogue", and he quotes part of a letter, the contents of which every hospital chaplain should take to heart. It reads,

> I often ponder over the nature of true human sincerity, true transparency. . . . It is a rare and difficult thing; and how much it depends on the person who is listening to us! There are those who pull down the barriers and make the way smooth; there are those who force the doors and enter our territory like invaders; there are those who barricade us in, shut us in upon ourselves, dig ditches and throw up walls around us; there are those who set us out of tune and listen only to our false notes; there are those for whom we always remain strangers, speaking an unknown tongue. And when it is our turn to listen, which of these are we for the other person's sincerity?

[1] R. C. Cabot and R. L. Dicks, *The Art of Ministering to the Sick* (MacMillan Co., New York, 1953) p. 208.

That should make us think of God, who is not only one who says, "Listen to me!" but also one who says: "I am listening to you." [1]

Such relationship can only be established when the chaplain is prepared to give time to the patient and help him express his feelings in an atmosphere of complete confidence and freedom.

Sensitive not superficial.   Often the chaplain, if he so wishes, can keep the patient at arm's length and so avoid any meaningful confrontation. He may be afraid of revealing his own inadequacies and failings, and their exposure is far too threatening for him. Consequently he contents himself with a superficial approach, confining the conversation to generalities and controlling the situation within limited boundaries. If this be the case, he will never be sensitive to the real needs of his patients and completely fail to see and listen to their feelings. His sensitivity must also be directed inwards to his own needs so that they do not disrupt the relationship and inhibit his approach, for he cannot listen to another if he is deaf to his own distracting concerns. Sensitive observation will only come by experience in ministering to those in need.

Servant, not status-seeker.   They who come to serve sick people will approach "not with eye-service, as men pleasers; but as the servants of Christ, doing the will of God from the heart" (Eph. 6.6). In an age when to so many people status seems a key word, and a concern for their "rights" the chief occupation of their minds, the hospital may be tempted to conform. When he wants to imitate some other role or adopt the prestige of some other office it is a tragic sign of his own inadequacy and insecurity. The quality of his life and service will prove of far more beneficial help to the patient than any quantity of recognition it might acquire.

"In quietness and confidence" and not in haste and pressure will the chaplain fulfil an adequate ministry, serving the sick with a professionalism which is concealed within his own person. *Ars est celare artem.*

[1] P. Tournier, *The Meaning of Persons* (S.C.M. Press, 1957) p. 165.

2

The Chaplain's Ministry
to the Patient

To the uninitiated a hospital can appear rather frightening. In an age of specialization so many different members of staff are involved in the total care of the patient, and as has been pointed out, "each hospital has a personality, a character of its own. . . . There is no Ministry of Health prototype, no external example, no textbook model, no platonic idea on which it can be fashioned."[1] In hospital one is confronted by the raw stuff of human existence and has to wrestle with the basic issues of life and death. Innumerable questions have to be asked which cannot be fully met apart from a religious understanding.

THE PATIENT IN HOSPITAL

There can be no generalizations, for each patient will react in his own way. Illness is an intrusion into the normal rhythm of his life. One thing is certain—he will be a different person from what he is when well. He will have been uprooted from his normal environment, separated from his friends and family, and brought into the day-to-day life of a hospital ward, "where boredom is interspersed with drama and tragedy, loneliness is relieved by the companionship of strangers, the hopefulness of the convalescent contrasts with the hopelessness of the dying, the strangeness of a new environment is succeeded by the security of a known routine, anxiety, hilarity and embarrassment

[1] R. W. Revans, *Standards for Morale : Cause and Effect in Hospitals.*

intermingle with monotony." [1] Although the hospital may be viewed as "authoritative and mysterious" yet it is seen by the majority of patients as a place where kindness and compassion reign and where miracles both of medicine and surgery occur. The patient may feel insecure in a strange bed in a strange place with strange people, yet he knows everything will be done to help and heal his sickness. His anxiety about hospital life probably has begun before his actual admission so when he eventually comes he has built up all sorts of fantasies and fears. Whatever emotions have been uppermost in his mind prior to becoming a patient will probably come into prominence during his illness, anxiety may be increased, feelings of guilt will be brought out into the open. If he sees illness as a punishment he will react to being punished, and so become resentful and angry. He will have fears of the unknown and of how he will respond to a new environment and to his loss of independency. His insecurity will be very marked until he knows those around him, builds up confidence in them, and eventually feels safe and secure. Very seldom is a person prepared for sickness; it often comes without warning and so frequently creates shock and crisis.

PAIN AND ITS EFFECTS

Pain usually draws a person within himself with an inability to concentrate on externals. The urge to self-preservation leads him to an excessive preoccupation with self, temporary loss of interest in other patients and people about him. When faced with such a crisis so often he becomes "cracked across by care" (Baudelaire). He feels so dependent upon others and inferior to the healthy around him. Feelings of embarrassment may arise when modesty is threatened in the frequent examinations and exposures which are often necessary for treatment. Most intimate functions have sometimes to be performed in the presence of other people who are often strangers. He is cut off

[1] A. Cartwright, *Human Relations and Hospital Care* (Routledge and Kegan Paul, 1964) p. 69.

and out of touch with others, and so feels isolated and apart on an island of pain, with a loneliness "that yet could not have been more complete anywhere—either at the bottom of the sea or under the earth" (Tolstoi). Some will tend to become bitter and resentful while others will be passive or submissive. Many repressed emotional problems emerge, for there is so much time to think. In acute pain the fear of death and the threat of "non-being" will fill some with apprehension and others with horror or panic. The very sights, sounds, and smells of the ward, together with all the complex techniques of surgery and medicine may on the one hand give him confidence yet on the other may equally increase his anxiety and fear. Often irrational fears arise together with irrational changes in behaviour. "Pain", wrote Daudet, "is always something new for him who suffers, but banal to those about him. They will all get used to it except myself."

Thoughts will generally be centred on the illness itself and its effects on oneself and others. Anxiety will arise until a satisfactory diagnosis is made. If there is to be an operation thoughts will arise about the anaesthetic or the possible post-operative discomforts. The length of stay in hospital will be of concern, as well as the welfare of the family at home, particularly if there are young children dependent upon a sick mother. The patient will also think about his work or his business concerns.

Feelings of guilt may arise: "Why did this happen to me?" "Is it my fault?", "Have I let the family down?"—and his thoughts will go back over the past. Uppermost in his mind will be the fear of pain or of some physical handicap or deformity. There may also be in his mind such questions as "Will they find I have cancer?", "Will they tell me the truth?", "Am I going to die?"

HOW THE PATIENT SEES THE CHAPLAIN

It is important for the chaplain to sense what his presence in the hospital symbolizes. It will of course mean different things

to different people, and he must respond accordingly, otherwise his pastoral care will soon become stereotyped. The inner
world of the patient must be an area he should explore with the
utmost discretion and tact, with a sensitivity which will not
pierce or hurt, and with interest rather than curiosity. He will
be alert to the hopes, fears, tensions, and needs of his people.

Many will see him in an entirely *authoritative role*, and there
will be little opportunity for a deep relationship to be established. Prayers might be recited and sacraments administered
but no person-to-person ministry established. There will be
chaplains who will be more secure cultivating such an image
for this very reason, for it can serve as a cloak to cover
inadequacies and conceal anxieties. There will of course be
times when the chaplain will need to exercise all the authority
of his priesthood, but if his approach be seen in the eyes of the
patient as one of domineering and dictating, this will only serve
to belittle and inhibit him, and block any flow of free conversation between them.

The chaplain may be hailed as a *miracle worker* whose prayers
and petitions have a somewhat magical effect and will manipu-
late the whole situation into what the patient wishes. They
have said their prayers and nothing seems to have happened
at all. Here comes one who cannot possibly fail! Unless this
attitude is rectified and misconceptions clarified much harm
can emerge, particularly when false hopes and expectations
are built up.

He may be seen as a *problem-solver*, to tell patients what they
are to do. "If you were me, what would you do, Vicar?" He
will find that it is a far more fruitful and productive exercise to
help them to answer their own questionings and promptings.
So easily can the chaplain be played off—quite unintentionally
sometimes—against the social worker or sister of the ward. At
all costs must the chaplain avoid a "Here's the answer—what's
your problem?" approach.

Patients will sometimes see him as so completely an *other-
worldly* figure that they feel he cannot possibly be aware of
down-to-earth problems or such seeming trivialities that

bother and concern them. So idealistic a personage is he, that he has probable never had to face any of the painful facts of life at all!

There are still many who view him in a *threatening and foreboding* light, and his presence as a rather ominous sign of their serious physical or spiritual state. The chaplain will soon sense this reaction, for either the patient will become so taciturn that real communication becomes a most difficult exercise, or such remarks as "I'm fine! There's nothing wrong with me. Old Mr A. is pretty bad down there!" make it evident as to the image conceived.

Fortunately there will be others who will see him as a *chaplain* who has come to exercise his priesthood within the hospital; one who will sense the patient's emotional mood and spiritual state and respond accordingly, who will "feel into" the patient's inner person and condition, binding up his brokenness that he may be whole again.

HOW THE CHAPLAIN SEES THE PATIENT

The reaction of the patient to his illness will depend upon his own individual personality, e.g. the independent and extrovert will not take kindly to being laid low and will therefore be more prone to worry and be irritated. Sick persons will be very sensitive to every word spoken, no matter how trivial. A sense of bravado may well camouflage deep-rooted fears, and induced cheerfulness may conceal acute depression.

In each patient the chaplain will see a person—a person who happens for the time being to be a hospital patient, and not vice versa. Each patient will be accepted as a person of worth and dignity, independent of any negative feelings he might have conceived. He is not "an emotional/physical condition with a label on it"! The chaplain will sense what help is being sought, what needs are being expressed. Who is this person? What does he feel his problem to be? What is he trying to convey? These are the questions he must ask. Otherwise the rebuke of Sherlock Holmes to Dr Watson will be his: "You see, but you do not observe!" Facing crisis as the patient is, he will often in a first visit by the chaplain reveal quite an amount of personal and intimate information. If this does happen the chaplain must not be surprised if during a second and subsequent visits the patient will become less talkative and probably seem more distant. As we have already seen, true communication between people lies deeper than words and the patient may feel over-sensitive and shy at having released so much personal information during a time of stress. Feeling is not always conveyed by words, and sickness is a time when people talk more readily and confide more easily, particularly to the chaplain whom they have never met before and will probably not see again. He may visit a patient only once or twice, but it is always at an impressionable time, for often the crisis of illness fosters an opportunity for growth.

The psychological effects of illness, with which the chaplain must be familiar, may take a positive form, e.g. humility, hope, humour, joy, faith—or they may create a negative reaction, e.g. fear, loneliness, guilt, resentment, boredom, regression. Many persons will recover far more readily physically than emotionally, for healing is something far greater than the mere curing of disease.

HOW THE CHAPLAIN SEES HIMSELF

The chaplain who sees others without being prepared to see himself will always prove ineffective. He cannot ask "Who is the patient?" before he has asked and attempted to answer the question "Who am I?"; he cannot come to others if he has not first "come to himself". Unless he is prepared to do this, he can either set up an image of himself and become identified with it (see above), or he can project himself on to the sort of image he feels he ought to be, and then spend his time in attempting to achieve it. On the other hand he can merely resign himself to his inability to establish his identity with any degree of satisfaction or success. When a chaplain knows who he is and what he really is about in the hospital situation, then

he is given the capacity and grace to bring health and wholeness into a sick community. Until then he will only breed
anxiety and further dis-ease.

He will come to the patient as a *pastor* to tend his spiritual
growth. He will encourage the sick person to talk to him, and
will put him at ease by the quietness of his approach and the
depth and sincerity of his interest. By his natural friendliness
he will lead the patient out of himself and away from his
morbidity and self concern. He will provide strength and
courage for those held captive to terror and to doubt. As pastor
his ministry will include bringing insight to those who are
blind to the real causes of their trouble and those who are
bruised by their own unavailing efforts to be free will be
comforted.

One of his most important roles will be that of *teacher*. Much
misunderstanding still exists about the whole ministry of healing, and his task will be to make plain before his people the
Church's teaching on the problems of sickness, disease, and
pain, of suffering and of death. He will teach them how to pray
and how the power of the risen Christ can be released to bring
solace and healing to those who are sick.

Time must also be spent in teaching his fellow clergy and
ordinands how to exercise an effective ministry to all who are
troubled and heavy-laden. If he is chaplain to a psychiatric
hospital this part of his work will have an added importance,
for much still needs to be done in this respect. Shame and stigma over mental illness and emotional problems are still rife,
and opportunity should be afforded him to exercise a real
teaching ministry among the members of the community.

Again, he will take his place in the teaching curriculum in
the school of nursing, participating in lectures and discussion
groups with both student and senior nurses, helping in this way
to relate Christian faith with nursing care and practice.
Opportunity will be afforded him to outline important features
of his own ministry and how chaplain and nurse can best co-
operate in their total care and concern for the patient. In the
small interdisciplinary discussion groups he may hold in the

hospital much can be taught, and various problems and difficulties can be worked through and resolved.

The chaplain comes to his people with the grace and authority of God, and so exercises the ministry of a *prophet*. "Thus saith the Lord" will be the introduction to his message, as he testifies to the fact of God's over-ruling power and love in a community which is concerned with various forms of suffering and pain. He will see himself as someone who has been called to fulfil a very special task in the whole work of healing, not only for individuals but for the spiritual life of the community which is the hospital. As a prophet he will proclaim the good news of the Gospel, "Come unto me, all ye that labour and are heavy-laden, and I will give you rest." There will be a number of patients who will have only a vague sense of God as Love, fearing him more than they trust him. To each he will bring faith for fear and reconciliation for estrangement.

He comes as an *evangelist* to interpret or articulate to those around him in hospital what God is like. If his ways are vague and uncertain then his speech will be trivial and his prayers meaningless and irrelevant. The "one thing needful" in his evangelistic ministry will be the growth and development of the personal spiritual life of each individual patient or member of staff. Every bedside visit, every service in chapel or ward, becomes an evangelistic opportunity, offering freedom from frustration and giving security to those undergoing the strain and stress of sickness.

In his preaching in the hospital chapel he will emphasize faith, understanding, and power in such positive terms that his congregation will not only hear what he says but will also feel what he means.

Much of the chaplain's time will be spent in administering the sacraments both in the chapel and on the wards, and at times of emergency or crisis. He will be seen as their *priest*. For them his bidding will be "Draw near with faith"; his command will be his Lord's, "Do this in remembrance of me". His priesthood will be exercised in an endless variety of ways throughout the day, and often long into the night. He it is who, together with the faithful members of his staff and community, leads his people to realize the presence of Christ in the very heart of their pain, bidding them see "in the case of Moses, the fire of divine charity burning in the midst of the thorns". When the sacramental ministry lies at the centre of hospital work, new life is released to work effectively within the bodies and souls of its patients, loosening crippling restraints and fostering conditions for health. Within a framework of a sacramental ministry in hospital both science and religion can work as creative powers side by side in a task which neither can accomplish alone.

THE INITIAL INTERVIEW

The patient is likely to experience some anxiety or apprehension when a priest or minister approaches the bedside. Sometimes it will be the first time he has spoken to a clergyman for years, so the chaplain should take the necessary steps to reduce any strainful factors involved. It is essential in the opening minutes to establish such a relationship as will open the way for free communication to take place. He will discern the mood and sense the feeling of the patient from postures, facial expressions, and tone of voice. He should attempt to realize what it means to the patient to be visited by a priest whom he has never seen before and probably never expected to see! He cannot assume that any particular patient will understand why the chaplain is there at all. If he does not take care to explain his presence to the patient the latter will only speak in generalities and see him as just another visitor among many. The defences of the patient will only serve as a barrier behind which he can protect himself; he will not feel at all himself until he discovers why the chaplain has called and what he is about. Rather than a vague and ambiguous greeting such as "Good morning. I'm the Anglican/Free Church/Roman Catholic chaplain", it will be far more meaningful to the patient if he takes trouble to make clear the purpose of his call. "Good morning, Mr Smith, I am the whole/part-time Anglican/Free

Church/Roman Catholic chaplain on the staff of this hospital. The chaplains work in full co-operation with the medical and nursing staff and other members of the hospital team in the total care of the patients. I shall be pleased to help you in whatever way I can. . . ." Such an illustration can obviously only serve as a guide and should not become a "set piece" repeated parrot-wise from patient to patient. Each chaplain will obviously have his own individual approach and method, and the way in which he expresses the purpose of his visit at the bedside of someone who has not sent for him. Without such an introduction, as we have seen, the patient will probably say only what he feels the chaplain wants to hear.

The chaplain will be careful however not to "over-structure" his opening remarks, for then their very structure becomes more important than their sensitivity, and "cold routine" takes the place of "warm concern". Real fellowship must first be established, for it is only then that empathy occurs. "It is impossible to understand another individual if it is impossible at the same time to identify one's self with him" (Jung). When questions have to be asked they will take up leads which have already been evident but perhaps inadequately expressed by the patient, and they should always be open and expansive rather than narrow and confined. The information which will be forthcoming will direct the chaplain to the most important areas of need, and it will be on those concerns that he will centre his pastoral care in subsequent calls.

Rather than use this initial interview to gain all relevant information and data he should see the first encounter as an opportunity to set up a helping relationship. If this happens then subsequent information will usually fall into place. Instead of using diagnostic skills the chaplain will work co-operatively alongside the patient, playing a supporting and listening role. It will be seen that in this way the sick person does not usually remain passive and dependent but active and creative. The best judge of his problems and difficulties will often be the patient himself, and he must be given every opportunity to express them in an open and permissive way.

The chaplain will then follow them to uncover and deal with the difficulties at hand and build the relationship around the issues and feelings which have been released and expressed by the patient. The initiative throughout the interview must so often lie with the sick person, and it is not for the chaplain to interject features which he feels are far more important. Rather must he develop and work through the issues which are raised at the pace set by the patient.

DIFFERENT CLASSIFICATIONS

Any attempt to classify has its dangers, but it is important for the chaplain to have insight into the needs of various types of patients. There can be no generalizations, for each will react in his own way, and any stereotyped approach must be avoided at all costs.

The surgical patient. It has been said that the questions which most frequently occupy the minds of surgical patients are: "Is it serious?"; "Is the operation dangerous?"; "Will I get well?"; "Am I going to die?" Such enquiries are naturally in the sphere of the surgeon's domain, but the chaplain can do much to relieve some of the patient's anxieties. He will need to have a clear understanding of some of these emotional reactions to surgery—"What will they find?"; "Will they tell me the truth?", etc. Coupled with such questions there may be the dread of anaesthetics and the fear of post-operative discomforts. Naturally so much will depend upon the explanation of the various procedures outlined by the surgeon beforehand, for the real relationship between surgeon and patient usually begins in the out-patients' department when they first meet together.

It must be remembered that there is no such thing as a "minor" operation to the patient; in his case it will always be "major". It is not helpful therefore to state that "I knew someone once who had exactly the same sort of operation", or "I had a similar thing myself".

Pre-operative stage. Before the actual operation the patient may feel a great sense of loneliness and isolation, coupled with the fear of the unknown. The chaplain's main concern will be to help the patient express what fears and dreads he might have. Here he can prompt when necessary, and ask how he feels about the operation. Where a supporting role is required the chaplain can build up confidence in the surgeon and his staff. If there are any signs of guilt feelings, of being afraid, or any feeling of shame, the chaplain can point to the naturalness of anxiety and so help the patient go to the operating theatre as calm and composed as possible. Prayers might be said, and laying on of hands and holy unction be administered (see Chapter 5). Again the assurance that he will be remembered in the hospital chapel or parish church at the time of the Eucharist or at the hour of the operation will do much to support and strengthen him. The most convenient time for visiting him will be the evening before the operation so that he may have as rested a night as possible and have nothing to disrupt the pre-medication given early the next morning.

Post-operative stage. Surgery often means a certain amount of dependency in the early post-operative stages. If the patient succumbs to a state of dependency he will be apt to make unnecessary demands on the nursing staff; if he reacts strongly against it, then he will often become irritable and difficult. Major surgery may often bring in its train a period of despondency of which the chaplain should be aware. During this post-operative stage visits should naturally be kept as brief as possible. Support might be needed for the family if major surgery has taken place. At this stage the very presence of the chaplain will be strengthening and supporting. Words will be kept at a minimum and physical touch, either the laying on of hands used informally with the blessing or the clasping of the patient's hand, will do much to bring a deep sense of peace and inspire confidence and the will to live.

The medical patient. Patients on the medical ward will need much reassuring. So many will have been on the ward for some time or have had to pay frequent visits to hospital. Many of them will be undergoing series of tests and observations, some of which can be rather unpleasant. Coupled with this is the fear of what these various tests and series of X-rays will reveal. Some patients will be suffering from stubborn and long-standing disorders, and live perpetually under the shadow of another attack which might prove fatal. Those with respiratory disorders can be very frightened when spasms of loss of breath occur, and experience many sleepless nights. The fear of being an invalid may be very real in their minds, or a life of dependency on others. There will be patients too who have been admitted to hospital as an emergency, and who will find it hard to reconcile themselves to this sudden disruption from family and social life to entry into a hospital ward utterly dependent and committed to enforced bedrest. Inevitable worries about home and business concerns will arise. It will be part of the chaplain's role to allay any signs of self-pity or morbid introspection, yet show sufficient sympathy and understanding in "feeling into" the fears and anxieties which are expressed. By being prepared to spend time at the bedside and help the patient to verbalize his feelings he will be doing much to comfort and support him.

The geriatric patient. It will be necessary for the chaplain to be familiar with some of the psychological, physiological, and sociological implications of old age, for he will then be aware of the behaviour patterns of the geriatric patients and the factors which cause them. Among the many fears in the minds of old people will be those of uselessness, loneliness, and despondency. The chaplain will help them to see that old age is far more than a negative state of being and that old people can still be creative in spite of failing physical powers. Far too often old people are offered charity and pity rather than a dignified participation in creative work. It will be part of the chaplain's task to pay frequent visits to the geriatric wards and be prepared to listen and to demonstrate God's love and interest, even though there may be no visible or verbal response. There will often be frequent repetition in their conversation, and reminiscing about the past. Any attempt to interrupt may cause them real anxiety and will sometimes break the relationship.

Often the chaplain will find that many such patients are shy, and yet are very anxious to make contact. There will be lapses of memory and other obvious signs of physical frailty and debility. Many geriatric patients have a simple but sincere faith with a deep sense of humility and serenity. One such patient once described her state as one in which "death takes little bits of me". Great patience must needs be exercised by the chaplain, for old people must not be hurried or given any sense of abandonment. For those who are acutely ill, reassurance will be the keynote of his ministry, and the instilling of confidence and encouragement. The long-term patient may be impaired both physically and mentally, and his ability to communicate may often be poor, but there will be many of the elderly whom the chaplain can lead to private acts of prayer and bible reading (if their eyesight is failing, the chaplain will read selected and familiar passages of scripture to them). They usually value periods of worship and appreciate a ward service. Nursing the infirm and incontinent can be a most exacting task and members of staff will need constant support and encouragement.

Many geriatric patients suffer from a loss of a sense of personal identity. Formerly they were probably figures of authority in their homes. Now they are wholly dependent upon others. They will treasure anything which will help them maintain a sense of selfhood. The transition from home to hospital creates much anxiety in their minds. The chaplain can be the much-needed bridge between hospital and the community, especially if he serves as a part-time chaplain and is familiar with the area in which the patient lived. He will be able to bring news of family and friends and home associations.

Emotional reactions will have to be watched, for old people

can often adopt an authoritative role to the young priest which may hinder any effective help he proffers. Conversely they may prefer to become extremely and helplessly dependent and compel far more attention than may be necessary or helpful. Dangers of both transference and counter-transference need to be watched, and the chaplain very much the master of himself in these situations.

The maternity patient. Opportunities for pastoral care abound on maternity wards. Few of the patients are ill in the official sense of the term, so the chaplain can have lengthier talks with the young mothers, although there will not be many convenient times for visiting. Apart from the normal ward routine there will be feeding times and rest periods, and the chaplain should adhere to the most suitable times for his pastoral calls. He will watch for appropriate opportunities to discuss Christian baptism, the care and upbringing of the child, and the importance of home life. It is often useful to have appropriate devotional literature for the young mother to take home.

Although the maternity ward has its joys and pleasures, yet there is often tragedy and heartbreak. The chaplain should always make discreet enquiries about mothers who have lost their babies so that he can avoid any embarrassment when visiting and also offer sympathy and condolence. The disappointment over the loss of a child will often find verbal expression in such questions as "Why has this happened to me?" The chaplain must be kept informed about the condition of babies and of any problems relating to the baby's father. It may not always be discreet to ask about the father.

Many maternity patients will fear that their baby will be stillborn or deformed or abnormal in some way or other. Their attitude to pregnancy will vary considerably from patient to patient. Some will long for a baby, yet there will be others who resent it. A few may be unmarried and faced with the problem of whether to keep the baby or have the child adopted. A number of expectant mothers will need weeks of rest in hospital prior to the birth of their child, and apart from monotony and

4

depression there will be the added concern about father and young children at home. There will be instances when the chaplain's advice will be sought on the ethical problems of abortion and sterilization.

In his pastoral care of the mother of a deformed child the chaplain will be aware of guilt feelings which often occur in the minds of such parents. Some may feel that they are entirely responsible for what has happened and that they are being punished for past misdeeds. Much spiritual support and comfort will be needed to help assuage the emotional shock and acute disappointment. The shame of the unmarried mother and the grief of the mother of a stillborn child will require all the sensitivity that the chaplain can muster, and it is always helpful if he can work in full co-operation with the medical social worker so that together the maximum amount of support and reassurance might be forthcoming.

The gynaecological patient.   In his visiting of gynaecological patients it is imperative that the chaplain should have the fullest co-operation from the doctors and nursing staff in order that he should know as much relevant information about each patient as possible. Only then will he be aware of the emotional and spiritual needs of those who have had miscarriages and abortions, and those who hope to increase their chances of motherhood. Medico-moral problems will be met with frequently, and the chaplain should be ready to give advice on such problems both to members of staff and to patients themselves. As with the maternity patient the chaplain and medical social worker should work together in dealing with such problems as arise on these wards.

The paediatric patient.   Being in hospital is a highly emotional and traumatic experience for a child. Up to the age of 3/4 his main anxiety seems to be that of separation from parents. Older children are more concerned with hospital procedures. One study group dealing with young children in hospital was presented with thirty essays on hospital . . . written at school by children whose average age was twelve years. Some of the children only knew hospitals from visits or hearsay, others had been patients. The group reported . . . they all expressed fear, mostly fear of operations, of not coming round from the anaesthetic, of the doctor making a wrong incision. The fear of those who had not actually been patients always seemed to be concerned with what it would be like to have an operation. Some of those who had been patients were still preoccupied with the fears that they had had *before* operation rather than with any post-operative experiences.[1]

The primary need of sick children in hospital is reassurance, and they will be quick to see through any façade and insecurity or uncertainty of approach. The chaplain's ministry will be expressed not so much in words as in what he communicates to them through his very presence with them. Children are quick to see what we really are and to sense our moods and emotions. The priest should read all he can about child psychology and so be ready to meet the varying emotional needs of those who are sick. He will find that symbolic acts prove a helpful part of his ministry. Physical touch, the clasping of the child's hand, and the laying on of hands in anointing or blessing do much to strengthen and reassure.

On paediatric wards the chaplain's ministry will be threefold—to the child, to his parents, and to the nursing staff who have the care of him. The illness of the child will always prove a time of much stress for the parents; so often a sense of guilt will be present: Is mother/father in some way responsible for what has happened? Should more care have been taken? Should they have sent for the doctor earlier? Although it may be extremely difficult at times, the emotions of the parents should be kept under control when they are at the bedside, for the child's anxiety and fear will be accentuated by those of the parents, and he will become increasingly upset, emotionally and physically. Parents should be encouraged by the chaplain to communicate their feelings freely in his talks to them and during his periods of counselling with them. It is not easy to

[1] E. Barnes, *People in Hospital* (Macmillan, 1961) p. 97.

remain objective where sick children are concerned, and nursing staff will need every support from the chaplain, particularly when religious doubts arise in their minds, for a children's ward is a school of theology. There are often emotional factors when, for instance, sick children adopt their nurses as "mother-substitutes". On the other hand, nurses themselves may become too possessive. The discharge of the child back home may prove most difficult and unsettling should these emotional involvements become acute. To nurse young children is no easy task, but the nurse will find it among her most rewarding and satisfying duties.

The cancer patient. Often cancer gives little warning of its presence, and the shock to the patient on discovering that he has the disease will need all the reassurance the chaplain can give. To many the very mention of "cancer" means a death-sentence, and one of the dangerous consequences of such reaction will be the loss of the will to live. Many will feel that they are in some way "abhorrent", "dirty", or "repellent". It will therefore be important to the chaplain's ministry to establish real contact with the patient, for there will be a strong need for companionship and relationship. Every encouragement should be given to help them talk about themselves. There will be some who will speak quite freely of their condition; others will react as if there were nothing seriously the matter and ignore the real truth.

It will always be wise to find out particulars about the medical or surgical condition from the doctor, and that there be a concerted approach from chaplain, doctor, sister, social worker, and family. Such teamwork will be essential.

The physically handicapped. The emotional reactions to being handicapped will need attention if the chaplain is going to offer help and support. There is often denial, or the hoping for a miraculous cure, such as the discovery of a new drug. Sometimes the chaplain will sense an underlying depression coupled with anger, resentment, and a sense of rejection. The most profitable service the chaplain can render is to stay with the patient, working through his disappointments and doubts, encouraging him to go forward, pointing out possibilities of creative work, and offering the full support of the community. In this way he will help him accept his disability and make the necessary readjustments to his life situation. To counsel effectively the chaplain will need to understand the limitations imposed by the physical handicap and its significance for the sufferer. Where there has been handicap caused by amputation of a limb, the whole symptomatology of grief and mourning will often come into play, for the loss of part of oneself, be it arm or leg, or a body-function, may produce similar reactions to that of the death of a loved one. The helpfulness of the chaplain will largely depend upon the confidence the patient has in him, and the more stability and maturity he can show the better and more secure the relationship will be.

The ministry to families and parents will be an important contribution to the chaplain's work with the patient. Parents may blame themselves for a child's deformity or feel it is a punishment for wrong-doing. There may be an unconscious rejection of the child or member of family. Feelings of guilt and shame may be evident and there will be need to talk these out, for the attitude of those about him will have a clear effect on the patient himself.

The orthopaedic patient. Orthopaedic wards are normally bright and cheerful, but confinement to bed for lengthy periods can often lead to bouts of depression and discouragement. Learning to walk again on stiffened joints and wasted muscles can be painful and frustrating. Patients will need every encouragement from the chaplain, and visits on such wards are normally much appreciated. As orthopaedic patients are usually not in general ill-health visits can be longer and more frequent.

Skin disorders. Patients who suffer from skin troubles are normally very sensitive about their condition and appearance.

The chaplain will often find that they have a deep sense of loneliness and clamour for love and acceptance. They feel they are in some way obnoxious and cut off, and it is important that the chaplain offer the companionship they need. There will be much scope for his pastoral care, for many such patients need emotional support and a real understanding of underlying problems.

The chronically ill patient. The chaplain must have a sincere appreciation of the condition and feelings of the chronically sick patient, who may have been on the ward for months, or who has had to return to hospital from time to time. Loneliness will often be one of the chief factors which will need watching, with consequent brooding and self-pity. Members of the local congregation can do much to combat such feelings by linking up the patient with interests in the community and paying frequent calls on the patient. This will help him to feel useful and needed again. If the patient is not too ill he may undertake an intercessory ministry and help to pray in a widening sphere of concerns (not necessarily for other sick people, for this can lead to introspection and morbidity). Such a person can lose hope rather quickly, so every encouragement and reassurance will be given him without any sense of over-optimism. Aggression might sometimes occur, and the chaplain should not feel threatened at this in any way, but rather accept it as one of the reactions caused by long and depressing sickness.

The critically ill patient. It is important for the chaplain to watch his own feelings, for if he is tense or insecure at the bedside it will not be easy for the patient himself to feel a sense of confidence or security. Many a patient will be unable to think clearly or speak rationally; many will not be aware of their true condition. Some may want to talk about their anxieties and have the chaplain present, whilst others will be unwilling to face their crisis and prefer to be just left alone. There may be guilt feelings about the past and a need to make a confession. The chaplain must be alert to all such signs and reactions.

Some critically ill patients feel that more ought to be done for them, and tend to become somewhat impatient. Bouts of severe depression are also common.

The chaplain's ministry will always begin where the patient is, establishing such a relationship that the patient feels free to express his feelings. He will help support his faith in himself, in others, and in God, and bring composure and calm so that what has to be faced can be met with complete faith and confidence. Visits should be brief, and the more familiar the prayers recited the more meaningful will they be to a patient who is in this state of illness. The laying on of hands and Holy Unction can be administered when necessary and at an appropriate stage in the chaplain's relationship with the patient.

The unconscious patient. The unconscious patient often seems to hear far more than is sometimes imagined. It is important therefore to be careful what is said at the bedside, and families and friends should be warned about this. Many a priest has had experience of the unconscious patient repeating some words of a familiar prayer said at the bedside, or echoing an "Amen". Long familiarity with the well-known prayers had become such a part of the patient that now they were proving a stronger tower of faith on the brink of death. Manual acts are of great value to such a ministry, and if the chaplain considers it desirable the sacrament of Holy Unction can be administered although the patient may be unconscious.

The dying patient. Communication will often be difficult with the dying patient, for there may be inability to speak distinctly or think clearly. If this is the case then the chaplain should take the initiative. Much help can be derived from reference to the patient's own parish priest, who will probably be far more familiar with him than the chaplain. He may more easily understand what the patient is attempting to say and more freely interpret various gestures, etc. Strange and new faces at the bedside often jar at such a time, and it is extremely important for the chaplain to establish a relationship with the patient before this stage in his illness has been reached. Contact is often most difficult when there has been very little opportunity for earlier preparation. Paul Tournier comments on this in *A Doctor's Case Book in the Light of the Bible*:

> I have always felt that my fault lay farther back, that it was less in this silence, which was after all imposed by charity, than in not having been able earlier, when the patient was not so near death, to establish close contact with him and to create that climate of spiritual fellowship without which the truth cannot be told. It is in speaking of the meaning of things that we enter into this fellowship, giving the patient opportunity of talking to us about the things that are weighing on his mind, long before he reaches the last extremity (p. 171).[1]

Some patients will seem consciously or unconsciously to deny that they are dying. Real facts do not seem to register, and the more meaningful the relationship between chaplain and patient the more openness there will be to reality. Such a relationship is far stronger than words. Co-operation with the doctor, nursing staff, and social worker will help to assure an understanding approach, and each will be aware of the other's role in their total concern for the patient. The chaplain will find that the dying person is usually very lonely, and closeness and companionship are among the greatest comforts that can be brought him. This sense of being together, the readiness to "watch and pray", will help make the gulf between the world of the living and the dead less lonely and terrifying. One's mere presence will mean much; one's sensitive responsiveness to the feelings of the dying will mean even more. His thoughts, his hopes and aspirations—as well as his doubts and despair—all need to be shared, so that he is accepted and valued, and thereby given "a faith to die with grace and dignity".

With sensitive concern the chaplain will exercise his sacramental ministry, which will be an important part of his whole expression of caring.

[1] S.C.M. Reprint, 1958.

The bereaved family. To minister to the bereaved is perhaps one of the most difficult tasks facing the chaplain. Such an intense and emotional experience will need to be handled and met with courage, poise, and sympathetic acceptance. Where there is intense shock any attempt at logical reasoning, explanations, or justifications by the chaplain are wholly out of place and will mean very little to a mind which is numbed and dazed. By "being there" he will symbolize his concern, his care, and his understanding. This physical contact will help far more than words.

Should there be pent-up feelings and an urge to weep, expression of these should be encouraged. Such an emotional release will be cathartic in itself, but only if handled with a skilled response to and acceptance of such feelings expressed. The full-time chaplain will have little opportunity to follow up the members of the family, and referring them to their parish priest will be an essential part of his ministry, for encouragement, spiritual reassurance, and the working through of reactions such as loneliness, guilt, hostility, and helplessness will need much time and will only play an effective part when emotional release has had full expression.

In whatever condition the chaplain finds the patient, he comes to minister to a total person, not one part of him termed "the soul". He must accept him as he is in the unity of his being, and see his ministry as predominantly a permissive one. He will see himself in the patient, not as the strong set against the weak or the healthy as against the sick, but as a fellow-sufferer struggling with some of the same problems and beset with some of the familiar difficulties. In offering the patient part of himself the chaplain will be giving something deeper than mere sympathy and stronger than mere words. It will be an identification "whose work is wholeness and whose name is love".

The aim of the chaplain's ministry will be to foster spiritual growth, being aware as he must of "the power of the new being of the Divine Spirit, which alone makes successful pastoral care possible" (Tillich).

RECORD OF PASTORAL CALLS

Patient's first names...................................... Surname......................

Home address.. Ward........................

Single ☐   Divorced ☐   Age..............

Married ☐   Separated ☐   Occupation..................

Religious Denomination: Church of England ☐
Free Church ☐
Roman Catholic ☐
Jewish ☐
Other ☐

Home/Parish Church..

Parish Priest/Minister..

Commendation received ☐   Date.............................

Date of Admission.................... Date of Discharge....................

Previous Admissions.......................... Dates.....................

Treatment: Medical ☐   Surgical ☐   Psychiatric ☐

VISITS (dates)

....

....

....

....

....

....

....

Sacraments: Laying on of Hands ☐
Absolution ☐
Holy Communion ☐
Holy Unction ☐

Family seen: Father ☐   Mother ☐
Husband ☐   Wife ☐
Son ☐   Daughter ☐

Referrals: General Practitioner ☐
Social Worker ☐
Community Resources ☐
Chaplains ☐
Others ☐

Commended to Parish Priest/Minister ☐   Date............

Present Pastoral Needs............

....

Future Pastoral Care ....

....

INFORMATION

Before he can minister effectively the chaplain must be fully informed about the patients whom he visits. The more understanding he has, the more he will have to offer. Such information must naturally be kept strictly confidential and only shared with the other members of the hospital team. Parish priests cannot expect the chaplain to betray such information without the full consent of the patients themselves. The chaplain should be supplied with the daily admission slips, lists of seriously ill patients and those who will be undergoing operations. In this way he will be as up to date as possible with any relevant information. He cannot demand to read case-histories, but if relationships are as they should be between the chaplain and the ward-sister or charge-nurse then he will be given as much information as he will require before setting out on his ward visitations. If opportunity offers he may be allowed to sit in on some of the ward reports, not because of morbid interest but to learn how to co-operate and communicate in an effective and efficient manner.

THE KEEPING OF RECORDS

If the chaplain's visiting is to be done with consistency and orderliness some system of recording his pastoral calls will be essential. This may take various forms and each chaplain will be able to devise his own outline and develop his own method. Such recording serves many purposes. As well as keeping the chaplain up to date in his visiting it is a constant reminder of what has occurred during previous visits, which patients were not able to be seen during a recent ward-round. A frequent consultation of such records will enable him to sense some of his capabilities and be aware of his limitations. Such efficient recording will bring a fresh understanding and a new insight into his work. A constant appraisal of his work will be at hand. Are his calls proving meaningful? Are they lacking in direction? If so, where? How can they be improved? Is far too much time being spent on certain wards with certain types of patients? Why? It has been said that "written words are like stairs. One foot rests firmly on the last step without danger of lapse while the other foot reaches up for the next." [1] Such records should be carefully filed and all information kept strictly confidential. (See outlined record card on pages 48–49.)

LEARNING FROM THE PATIENT

"The greatest good we can do for others is not to give them what we have, but to show them how much they have to give." Often roles will become reversed—the patient will become the chaplain, the chaplain the patient. Ability to learn from each patient will be one of the finest gifts the chaplain can cultivate. If he has eyes to see he will perceive God at work in the courage and heroism of the pain-stricken, in the gratitude of the helpless, in the mumblings of the mentally ill. True pastoral care is always mutual and becomes a learning process for both involved. Allowing the priest to share in his very pain and sorrow, the patient gives far more than he is ever aware of, and teaches lessons which cannot easily be taught outside the sphere of the sickroom. "The poor sufferer whom I help confers a favour on me", writes Alan Richardson, "not I on him, because he shows me Christ, makes Christ real to me, enables me to touch, handle, tend, and serve Christ." [2] Blessed indeed is the chaplain who realizes this.

[1] Cabot and Dicks, *The Art of Ministering to the Sick* (Macmillan Co., New York, 1953) p. 255.
[2] Alan Richardson, *Theology of the New Testament* (S.C.M. 1958).

3

The Chaplain's Ministry to the Staff

The chaplain is concerned not only about the wholeness of the patient, but also about the wholeness of the hospital and its community. It will be one of his most important contributions as chaplain to see that good working relations are fostered; for all who tend the patient, or who are connected in any way with his restoration to health, are members of the Church, the Body of Christ, carrying out the redemptive work of Christ in a sick world. It will be part of his ministry to cultivate and encourage contacts with various members of the staff, for the effectiveness of his own ministry will depend to a great extent on their co-operation and support. He will endeavour to be in touch not only with "key" members but also with those who perhaps are not seen in so prominent a position, e.g. porters, domestic workers, ward-maids, etc. No matter what type of hospital it is in which he ministers, the chaplain will find that it will be, in varying degrees, an ever-changing population; new people coming and going and fresh problems frequently arising. To all whom he meets it will be his endeavour to show what God is like, interpreting to each the true end of the community in which they minister—the glory of God.

THE MEDICAL STAFF

Hospital chaplains are in a key position to foster good working relationships between Church and Medicine. Before active co-operation can be established the chaplain must be adequately trained for his task in hospital (see Chapter 8) and it is premature to conceive of him as a member of the healing team without such a most necessary preliminary. This is even more important and vital if the priest is to work in a psychiatric hospital, where he can make a positive Christian contribution to the various problems involved. Until he knows *why* he is there and what his real function is, and becomes proficient in its fulfilment, he cannot expect the consultant or registrar to seek his help and advice about the various patients under their care.

At present it is all too easy for the chaplain to be seen as an "extra" rather than an essential part of the hospital team, appearing on the side-line while the "real" work is being done by the doctors, nurses and others.[1] Far too often each goes his separate way. Sometimes he can feel completely out of place because of the rather possessive attitude adopted towards the patient by others. Under present circumstances he must therefore win his way and prove his worth. This he will do not by words but by deeds, by listening patiently and by learning gradually as he sets about to win the approval and trust of those around him.

The keynotes of his ministry to members of the medical team will therefore be *confidence*, *communication*, and *co-ordination*. Once he has gained the confidence of the medical staff much will be achieved in their total care of the patient. If this is not forthcoming then the chaplain will always feel anxious and insecure, threatened and defensive, so thwarting much of any idea of teamwork. Communication will depend on many factors and raises the question of how much medical, surgical, psychiatric knowledge the chaplain should have. If doctor and chaplain are to have any meaningful confrontation, each must be aware of and have understanding of the other's language. Whilst it is important for the chaplain to be familiar with

---

[1] Cf. Reinhold Niebuhr: "Sometimes when I compare myself with these efficient doctors and nurses hustling about I feel like an ancient medicine man dumped into the twentieth century. I think they have the same feeling toward me that I have about myself!"

medical terminology and the various techniques used in the general hospital, and the understanding of the psychiatric vocabulary and the various different forms of treatment in the psychiatric hospital, it is equally essential for physician, surgeon, and psychiatrist to familiarize themselves with the whole ministry of the chaplain and the "instruments" which the Church itself uses to make its approach effective in full co-operation with theirs. The chaplain must often take the initiative and make himself known to his medical colleagues, for they can be reticent and shy towards him, not being at all clear as to his place in the hospital and his part in the team. They often see no vital relationship between his work and their own.[1] There should be opportunity for the chaplain to be a member of the medical mess, for here mutual understanding and trust can be fostered. The value of such informal contacts cannot be over-emphasized.

Good communication will lead on to effective co-ordination. As soon as the medical staff are aware of the chaplain's work mutual discussion can take place. It is of extreme value to the priest if he is permitted to attend and participate in ward- and case-conferences, where not only clinical matters are discussed, but social and ethical problems are raised. The last word about the patient and his treatment will always rest with the doctor and his medical team, but the chaplain will have much to contribute to the total concern of the patient if he has been conscientious in his visiting, in his co-operation with the staff, and in his knowledge of certain features of the illness and the patient's emotional and spiritual reactions. Where such a

[1] See *Clergy Doctor Cooperation: A Report* (C.I.O., 1963), p. 6: "The Working Party has found no evidence of any systematic, or even organized, attempt to introduce medical graduates to the field of common action of clergy and doctors, nor any training that bears upon spiritual life. This finding, however, need not occasion surprise because it is true in general that post-graduate medical training is conceived almost invariably in terms of a narrow speciality. It does mean that however ill-informed the clergy may be about the life and attitudes of doctors, more especially on the psychological side of their work, doctors in their professional capacity are even less informed about the clergy."

relationship exists, only rarely will any major difficulty arise from their work together. Both will be ready to listen to the other; to learn from each other and work alongside each other for the wholeness of the patient's health, environment, and relationships. Peaceful co-existence will then soon develop into active co-operation.

It is to be hoped that the chaplain will be invited to take his part in the teaching programme of medical students, helping them to fulfil the vocation of a Christian doctor, and teaching some of the principles involved in a theology of medicine. Unfortunately very little if any opportunity for such common dialogue and teaching exists in the medical schools' curricula.[1] A recent memorandum submitted by a Joint Committee of the Churches' Council of Healing, the Institute of Religion and Medicine, and the Guild of Catholic Doctors to the Royal Commission on Medical Education, and published in *The Practitioner*, July 1967 (Vol. 199, pp. 78–82) states:

A questionnaire sent by The Institute of Religion and Medicine to the medical schools in England and Wales, asking what was done about teaching students how to understand patients' religious attitudes, how to cope with the dying and with various ethical problems, and whether the chaplain took any part in teaching, received fourteen replies. Of these only three felt able to complete the questionnaire; one of these estimated that three hours, and one, five hours, were spent in three years on these subjects; the third could not assess the time. The remaining eleven replied that there was no specific or regular teaching, or apparently any agreed policy on them, but that they were left to individual consultants, and that students had opportunities for discussion. Some seemed confident that such opportunities were taken; more seemed to doubt whether this was so. We feel strongly that this should not be left in doubt.

In four schools, the chaplain took some part (one at the students' request); one other was considering this; in four he took no part; five failed to answer the question.

[1] The lecture courses organized by the London Medical Group do much to remedy this defect. For a study of medico-moral problems, see *Ethics in Medical Progress*, ed. G. E. W. Wolstenholme and Maeve O'Connor (J. & A. Churchill, for the Ciba Foundation, 1966).

Included in its conclusions is the following recommendation:

> Medical education at some point must include teaching and testing
> on psychology, sociology, moral philosophy, and the philosophy of
> religion. There should be integration in the teaching of the struc-
> ture, function and purpose of man. Without this the student be-
> comes handicapped by a disproportionate interest in the organic
> side of medicine and finds it difficult to readjust his thinking and to
> retain his initial sense of vocation.

Unless such teaching is given no true healing can be offered
to the patient who once exclaimed, "Doctor, you may not be
aware of it, but my biggest problem was not that I was going
to die. It's what to do with my life now that I've recovered."
The illness will be cured, but not the patient.

THE NURSING STAFF

It is the nurse who spends the greatest amount of time with the
patient and has therefore much opportunity of understanding
his various emotional needs as well as his nursing care. Good
relations between the chaplain and the sister and her ward
staff are therefore essential. Their advice will be sought about
the various patients he will be visiting on the ward. Often
because of lack of time it will be on such information that he
will be able to select those patients who need his ministry
most, not of course ignoring or passing others by without some
acknowledgement made. In turn the chaplain will show the
staff how he will be able to help them; that he is ready to be
used and sent for at all times of day or night. The staff will
know that they can call for him when a family needs support;
when the patient is very ill or is to undergo an operation, or is
fearful, friendless, depressed, anxious, etc., and also when
there are personal problems or difficulties to be talked through
and discussed.

Along with his fellow-chaplains he will welcome all new
nurses on arrival at the hospital. It may be useful to send each

a letter of welcome from the chaplains, which will await them on their first day in the teaching school. With his Free Church, Roman Catholic, and Jewish colleagues he will participate in the teaching syllabus of the introductory course in the School of Nursing as well as in "block study" and "in-service training" programmes. The religious persuasion of nurses is now a personal and private matter for the nurse herself, and application forms do not usually include a question about this. "If it is desired to put student nurses in touch with church or other representatives of their particular denominations, an offer to do so could be conveyed in general terms to all (nurses)." [1] It is far more beneficial to make such talks as informal as possible and to break down the classroom atmosphere, in which very few nurses feel completely free to participate in open discussion. If such an informal structure cannot be arranged it might be helpful to suggest that written questions be submitted, anonymously if necessary, so that both chaplains and nurses can work through these in a meaningful and constructive way. More *exploration* and less *exhortation* perhaps sums up this approach. A corporate Communion might be arranged at the end of each introductory course, or a service of dedication prior to the student commencing her official duties as a nurse on the ward. This helps to impress on the young nurse the responsibilities she is now about to undertake and the necessity for spiritual support to undergird all her nursing techniques and methods. Commendations received from parish priests about the admission of new nurses from the parish are of immense help, particularly since the issue of the Ministry memorandum mentioned above presents certain difficulties in this direction.

There are two basic needs confronting the young student nurse—*security* and *stability*—and apart from any official programme of talks in the school of nursing the chaplain will take every opportunity of placing himself at the disposal of the nurse for personal guidance and help. It is time-consuming, but it

[1] See Memorandum, issued by the Ministry of Health: *Religious Persuasion of Nurses.*

should never be neglected. As well as dealing with other people's problems she will have difficulties of her own and she cannot deal adequately with the former unless she has had help in resolving the latter. A nurse of today works in an ever-changing society. Not only do patients change so rapidly, but her friends change, the doctor changes, her ward changes, and her hospital changes if she nurses in a group-hospital or if she is seconded for training elsewhere. If the chaplain is known to her, at least she will be able to see him, and in the services in the hospital chapel find a sense of continuity and a source of strength.

Senior nurses, too, will need the chaplain's care and attention. The work of senior administrators and educators in the nursing profession is now far more challenging and demanding than perhaps ever before, taking place as it does amid complex changes and modern developments. There are now far more demanding and intricate decisions to be taken. The time taken up in the day-to-day machinery of management leaves less and less opportunity to discuss various problems with both other staff members and patients. In addition there are the difficulties arising from shortage of staff, more part-time nurses and less full-time staff being resident in hospital.

The chaplain will arrange suitable times for chapel services in conjunction with the matron's office and make every effort to support the sense of vocation of the nurse, for a regular rule of life will meet with constant interruption, and it will not always be possible for her to maintain any regularity of worship. The constant problems of suffering and pain will daily beset her and she is exposed to strains and stresses which were not apparent to some of her seniors. A link-up with their neighbouring churches for those who are non-resident is extremely important, for not only does this strengthen spiritual ties, but it also breaks down the great problem of loneliness facing many of the nursing profession today. The co-operation of the parochial clergy and members of their congregations can do much to support the chaplain's ministry in this respect.

Every opportunity must be given for discussion between the

chaplain and the nursing staff. Various organizations[1] are at work in hospitals to help cater for the nurses' spiritual needs, but there is an important place for open discussion groups, not specifically confined to "Christian nurses", where problems can be brought out and ideas and difficulties shared. Much friendship and fellowship will be fostered in this way. It is not fully recognized how difficult it is for a young nurse to face up to questions of pain and death which would tax the most experienced Christian layman.

> The problem of suffering, the care of the dying, the ethics of euthanasia, abortion and sterilization; personal relationships with colleagues senior and junior, involving questions of status and authority; the affront to personality when a junior nurse trying to comfort a patient is told by a senior 'there's no time for that sort of thing'; the problem what to tell the patient; the keeping alive of people who are virtually corpses . . . Any nurse could compile a list of what has hit her, and the older and wiser the nurse, the longer her list . . . anyone can give an injection . . . but it takes a real person to comfort the bereaved . . .[2]

Some may become hardened and objective whilst others will tend to be too emotionally involved. A few will see a way out in developing a negative type of life or will leave hospital altogether. It is evident that there will be much scope for the chaplain's counselling ministry, which should be done quietly and informally rather than as a programme of official office hours for "interviewing".

Both in his official programme in the school of nursing curriculum and in his informal meeting and groups, the chaplain will be able to encourage for discussion some of the nurses' own topics rather than superimpose any deeply theological issues which can so easily develop into "another lecture from

---

[1] See list in *Christianity and Nursing Today*, A Report of a Working Party appointed by the Nurses' Christian Movement to study Christian work amongst nurses (Epworth Press, London, 1964) pp. 14–21 and Appendix D.

[2] Ibid., p. 24. See also *To the Anglican Nurse* (C.I.O. Revised Edition, 1967).

the chaplain". Time can be spent most profitably on such subjects as sex ethics, personal relationships, medico-moral problems (prolongation of life, abortion, euthanasia, sterilization), Christian marriage, the patient as a person, witnessing in a secular society, intercessory prayer, the healing ministry (and the nurse's contribution to it) suffering, death, bereavement, ministering to the family.

ADMINISTRATIVE STAFF

Not only must the chaplain seek co-operation with and exercise pastoral care of those whom he constantly meets on the wards; he must do the same also with those who minister behind the scenes to keep the administrative side of the hospital working efficiently. Every opportunity should be taken to meet the various heads of the different departments from time to time, both formally at staff meetings and informally over meals or at social functions at the hospital. Lunch hour services arranged in the hospital chapel provide further opportunities for worshipping together. Staff services, special services at St Luke's-tide, also enable many to come together who otherwise perhaps would not meet each other in a large community.

In some hospitals the chaplain is invited to say prayers at the commencement of meetings of the Board of Governors or Hospital Management Committees, and also to submit a written or verbal report of his work. In this way the members of the respective committees can more easily appreciate what the ministry of the chaplain actually involves and all that is implied in the pastoral care of a large hospital with its staff and patient population.

MEDICAL SOCIAL WORKERS

Over recent years much attention has been given to doctor/clergy co-operation, but very little study has been devoted to the relationship of social worker and priest, though there is much overlap in their respective ministries. Dr Kathleen Jones describes some of the differences of approach between the two professions thus:

> A sensitive spiritual counsellor . . . works in two dimensions, and and the social worker professionally only in one. The social worker is concerned with the here and now, and does not look beyond the human life-span, or the effect of one generation of a family on the next. The priest works at once in the temporal and the eternal. The drabbest and most unpromising parishioner is potentially "a child of God and an inheritor of the Kingdom of Heaven".[1]

Dr. J. S. Heywood sees "compassion" and "disciplined self-awareness" as the two "bridge areas" where both priest and caseworker meet. The writer reminds the priest of two of his most fundamental gifts which he has to bring to his people— "a meaningful understanding of prayer and the symbolism of the sacraments". "Case-work", she continues, "is concerned with helping people to cope with a specific problem. The priest is concerned with man's coping with the whole life, and understanding its meaning and purpose."[2]

Both chaplain and social worker must work together, and have a clear understanding of their approach to the patient. In many instances the chaplain will need the co-operation of the social worker in order to make his own ministry to the patient wholesome and meaningful; there will also be opportunities when the social worker will wish to turn to the chaplain for spiritual advice and guidance in dealing with particular professional problems. Each chaplain should be familiar with the social agencies in the area, and if he serves in a part-time capacity he can often supply relevant and valuable information about the family and home background of the patient. If he has a knowledge of psychology and an understanding of case-work techniques he will be more able to appreciate and co-operate with the work of the social service department.

---

[1] Dr Kathleen Jones, *The Compassionate Society* (S.P.C.K.) p. 39.
[2] Dr J. S. Heywood, *Casework and Pastoral Care* (S.P.C.K.). See also *Crucible* (C.I.O.) March 1968, pp. 33–34.

OVERSEAS STAFF

A large number of overseas staff are now working in English hospitals. So easily they can become isolated, lonely, and cut off from fellowship and friends on account of the difficulties of language and differences of custom. The chaplain will be ready to welcome them and work in co-operation with the parochial clergy in order to incorporate them as soon as possible into the general life of the community. The part-time chaplain will be able to arrange for them to find a welcome in the homes of the parish and link them, should they so wish, to the various church organizations.

STUDENTS

If the hospital is a teaching school there will be various students gaining experience in different departments—social work, dentistry, radiography, physiotherapy, etc.—quite apart from the large number of medical students. Although not officially members of the hospital staff, they will all be included in the pastoral care of the chaplain during their time in hospital. The majority of these will be non-resident, and here again their link with the community will be important. Many may be shy of encountering the chaplain, and commendations from their respective parishes or former hospitals will do much to provide an early contact. Information relating to the various denominational and interdenominational groups and organizations in the hospital and community can be supplied to them, and their participation encouraged in whatever discussion groups might be held.

VOLUNTARY HELPERS

A Ministry of Health circular HM(62)29 issued on 12 April 1962 gives advice on ways in which voluntary help in the hospital can be expanded, and asks hospital authorities to review the position and to arrange meetings with representatives of the appropriate voluntary organizations. It makes mention of services which can be provided by a League of Friends (The National Association of Leagues of Hospital Friends, 7 Grosvenor Crescent, London, S.W.1) and in paragraph II states:

> The Minister suggests that there should be continuing meetings with the representatives of the voluntary organizations which take responsibility for providing help at particular hospitals, so that current working and development of the services can be discussed and any improvements or extensions made. The hospital chaplains should be invited.

Although such helpers are not regarded as hospital staff the chaplain should work co-operatively and supportively with them, for they can be of great practical help. A list illustrating some of their services given in hospitals, including conveying of patients to and from the chapel and assisting in secretarial work etc., is included in the Ministry circular.[1]

Among other staff to be mentioned are the records' officer and admissions office staff (who are able to keep the chaplain supplied with day-to-day admissions and discharges and other relevant information about patients' allocation), the switchboard telephonists, and the domestic supervisors and their staff, all of whom help in the functioning of the hospital. The chaplain should be known to all and a friend of all.

LAY MINISTRY

It will be quite an impossible task for even a wholetime chaplain to minister adequately to both staff and patients. To this end as many of the staff as possible can be shown how each can exercise a lay ministry in the hospital. With the chaplains themselves working together as a team, much can be achieved with a well instructed nucleus of staff co-operating together.

[1] See also *A King's Fund Report: The Hospital Chaplain: An Enquiry into the Role of the Hospital Chaplain* (published by King Edward's Hospital Fund, 14 Palace Court, London, W.2, 1966) Chapter 4, pp. 32f.

More chaplains are needed, it is true, but many of the present practical difficulties can be resolved by more Christian doctors, more Christian administrators, more Christian nurses being a serving, caring, healing, therapeutic community within the hospital. Such leaders, who have first of all been made aware of some of the needs and problems and then taught how to meet them, can share and complement the ministry of the chaplain, meeting together, thinking together, and praying together. Such a lay ministry would entail serious rethinking of such terms as "status", "authority", and the whole hierarchical structure of the hospital. Many parochial schemes might be put into action; for example, "The People Next Door" of the parish can equally apply to the person in the next bed or the staff in the next department; the "street warden" can become the key figure of the hospital ward or unit, and so on. The relevance of the Christian faith would soon become evident, and within the hospital the living Church, which is the Body of Christ, would be seen in action, loving, healing, redeeming, and sanctifying. So, too, the true concept of the chaplain's ministry to the staff would be not so much to encourage them to help him in his work, but rather that he himself should help them, the whole community of God, to be in turn the Church in hospital. Pastoral care in hospitals could then be far *more* the total ministry of the Body of Christ and far *less* the special ministry of the individual chaplain.

4

The Chaplain's Ministry
in the Chapel

If the chaplain is to fulfil an adequate ministry in any large hospital he must be provided with the proper facilities and equipment to carry out his work. The Ministry of Health circular HM(63)80 recommends that there should be in each hospital a chapel or room set apart to serve as a chapel, which should be made available by mutual arrangement for the services of any of the denominations who wish to use it, and that whatever accessories of worship are required by each should be provided. Where there is a chapel it should be not only centrally situated but also attractively designed and kept open day and night for prayer and meditation. Ideally it should have sufficient space either at the back or along the aisle for beds and wheelchairs. Careful consideration should be given to the selection of comfortable seating accommodation so that there will be the least possible physical strain on patients during times of official services. The chapel should be architecturally and decoratively light and bright, symbolizing life, hope, and healing. Particularly is this important in large psychiatric hospitals. The majority of hospital chapels will be "dedicated" buildings and regulated by the Extra-Parochial Ministry Measure 1967.[1] In the few cases where the chapels are "consecrated" their use is restricted to Church of England services only, except with the sanction of the diocesan bishop.

---

[1] See *Order of United Service for the Dedication of a Hospital Chapel*, drawn up under the auspices of the Hospital Chaplaincies Council by a Joint

On 27 August 1965 the Ministry of Health sent recommendations to all Secretaries of Regional Hospital Boards and Boards of Governors about the design, planning, and equipment of new hospital chapels.[1]

The hospital chapel should be the centre of regular corporate worship for both staff and patients, the focal point of the whole hospital community, and be linked as far as possible to the life of the Church in general. The care and upkeep of the chapel will be in the hands of the hospital authorities. In some hospitals the Assistant Matrons' office will attend to the altar linen, laundry, and flowers, although this might also be seen as one of the duties of the voluntary organization mentioned in the previous chapter.

There might well be a small chapel committee functioning in a purely advisory capacity with a membership consisting of the chaplains, matron, house governor or hospital secretary, and one or two representatives of various departments. Items relating to the hospital chapel, its worship and its witness, as well as purely practical matters, can be discussed.

DEVOTIONAL LITERATURE

It will be found useful to have a selection of devotional literature for both staff and patients available at the back of the chapel, either in a tract case or displayed openly on a table. Such literature should be wisely chosen and attractive in form. Print should be large, so that patients can read without undue strain. Suitable literature is available from the Guild of St Raphael, 77 Kinnerton Street, London, S.W.1, from the Guild of Health, Edward Wilson House, Queen Anne Street, London, W.1, and from The Bible Reading Fellowship. (See selection in Appendix C.)

Committee of representatives of the Anglican, Roman Catholic, and Free Churches, and approved by the three Church Authorities (C.I.O., 1966).
[1] See *A King's Fund Report: The Hospital Chaplain* (published by King Edward's Hospital Fund, 1966), especially Chapter 3 and Appendix G.

CHAPLAIN'S OFFICE

It is recommended in the Ministry of Health memorandum HM(63)80 that "whenever possible, a room should be set apart for the chaplain's interviews etc., and secretarial facilities should also be provided". This is equally applicable to part-time chaplains, for it is essential that there should be a convenient room put at the disposal of the chaplains in order that they may see members of staff or patients privately. In the psychiatric hospital in particular much of the chaplain's time is taken up with individual counselling of patients. Such a room should be centrally situated and easily accessible for families who may wish to see the chaplain at various times.

Where it is not possible to obtain official secretarial help, the chaplain will probably have to rely on voluntary assistance. If this is so, he must assure that all medical information concerning the patients' condition be kept strictly confidential. The office should be equipped with desk, both internal and external telephones, filing cabinets for records and confidential material, typewriter, etc., with access to a duplicator. Comfortable chairs should be available for those who come to consult the chaplain, and the more informal the atmosphere the better.

Should such a room be available it is important that it be kept in good order and records efficiently and carefully filed. Ideally it should be near the chapel and the visitors' room.

CHAPEL FINANCES

The Extra-Parochial Ministry Measure 1967 repealed the Private Chapels Act 1871, and in Sub-section 2, paragraph 3, states with reference to "any university, college, school, hospital, or public or charitable institution . . . whether or not it possesses a chapel":

The alms collected in the course of or in connection with such offices and services shall be disposed of in such a manner as the

minister performing the office or service, subject to the direction o
the bishop of the diocese, may determine.

However, this ruling applies only to alms received by a clergyman of the Church of England and does not affect alms
collected by any other clergyman who may be appointed
chaplain to minister to patients of his own denomination.

The chaplain has therefore complete discretion as to the
purposes for which the chapel alms are spent, subject only to
any direction the bishop may give. Neither hospital authorities
nor chapel committees may decide the disposal of the alms.
Alms bags are among the accessories provided out of exchequer
funds. If there are permanent collecting boxes at the chapel
doors, it should be made clear that these are not to provide for
maintenance of the chapel, which is the responsibility of the
hospital authority. If the chaplain keeps the money in a bank
account it is convenient to nominate one person, preferably a
regular worshipper in the hospital chapel, to have power to
draw on the account in his absence.

Clearly the chaplains should not spend the alms on any items
which are to be provided by the hospital authorities. Other
accessories of worship could properly be purchased with the
alms, if the hospital is unable to provide them. Many chaplains
spend the alms on literature and equipment for pastoral and
evangelistic work in the hospital, as well as on strictly charitable
concerns. Whenever possible, the object to which the alms are
to be given should be decided and announced beforehand.
This can stimulate interest in the Church overseas, and in a
wide field of Christian and charitable activity.

Money handed to the chaplain by patients who receive Holy
Communion on the wards is usually intended as communion
alms, and should be so treated. However, the chaplain should
not receive any money which is said to be "for the hospital".

Particularly in psychiatric hospitals there may be some
patients who are subject to the Mental Health Act or other
forms of legal protection. If such patients are allowed to carry
money, this can only be because they are capable of handling

it. However, the chaplain must always be ready to act on the advice of the legal or medical officer responsible for such patients if any question arises about their almsgiving.

MORTUARY CHAPEL

The chaplain should visit the mortuary chapel regularly and see that it is as properly and reverently maintained as the hospital chapel itself. Families and friends may wish to view a deceased relative and prayers can be said with those who are bereaved. Far too often such chapels seem to be neglected and it should be one of the main concerns of the chaplain to liaise with the mortician and the hospital authorities and see that everything is done to keep the chapel in good and decent order.

Hospital Building Note 20: Mortuary and Post-Mortem Room (Ministry of Health, London, H.M.S.O., August 1933, reprinted with amendments, 1966) has relevant information about a "viewing room", in paragraphs 54, 55, and 57, as follows:

54. This is to enable bodies to be viewed by relatives and friends. It should be treated in a simple manner, so that it can be used by all religions and denominations. Exceptionally an additional viewing room may be necessary for particular denominations.
55. A draped trolley is now regarded as more hygienic and practical for viewing purposes than a fixed bier. The room should be attractively decorated and subdued lighting is recommended.
57. Visitors' waiting room. Visitors will wait here before going into the viewing room. Viewing times will generally be arranged so that unrelated parties do not overlap. It should be pleasantly furnished as a sitting space.

CHAPEL SERVICES

Where there is a whole-time chaplain the daily office can be recited at a time when members of the staff and perhaps a few patients can participate. In some hospital chapels there can also be a daily celebration of Holy Communion or an informal brief morning and evening service. Such a daily offering of prayer and liturgy helps to make the chapel the centre of the spiritual life of the hospital. When patients make up the majority of the congregation the length of the service is important, for sick people easily tire. Normally such services would not exceed half-an-hour's duration. On the other hand, those held in a psychiatric hospital can take the normal form of Matins and Evensong or a Sung Eucharist, for the majority of patients will be up and about. The most convenient times for services will largely be dependent upon the local situation and circumstances. The chaplain should discuss such arrangements with the matron and other officers so that hours of service do not clash with hospital routine and with the nurses' hours of duty. It will be imperative that service times be strictly observed.

TYPES OF SERVICES

As regards the exact type of services arranged on Sundays and weekdays the chaplain may wish either to base their structure on a shortened form of Matins or Evensong, or to use a completely informal service, comprising confession, absolution, versicles and responses, lesson, short address, prayers, hymns, and blessing. In both instances the permission of the bishop should be sought.

The service should be printed in large print on a card or leaflet which can be used by the congregation. In a large hospital with an adequate number of staff it might be possible to form a choir of nurses and medical students, and arrange regular choir practices. The more familiar the hymns the better, but they should always be most carefully selected. The chaplain can use his discretion about introducing modern tunes. Where the congregation is fairly static, such as in a psychiatric hospital chapel, new hymn tunes can be readily introduced. The address should be brief—about ten minutes—

and adapted to meet the needs of those present. Much instruction can be given in simple statements of gospel truth, for many who attend services in a hospital chapel are not regular churchgoers in the community. There should be emphasis on the gospel as the good news of redemption and salvation, translated into terms which are both meaningful and creative. For all concerned any tendency to speak down to patients, particularly in a psychiatric hospital, must be avoided at all costs. Generally speaking the chaplain will deliver his address as if under normal circumstances. Its content must speak to the fears and anxieties of those patients who attend. Many of such themes will be taken up as a result of his visiting on the wards and his discussions with staff etc. There should not be an over-emphasis on sickness and sin etc., but a clear message of hope, love, and thanksgiving. Patients will be informed about the times of services and full information can be given in the leaflets distributed to all patients on admission.

HOLY COMMUNION

A whole-time chaplain will normally be able to arrange Holy Communion services early in the morning for day staff coming on duty and another for night staff who have finished duty. In a large hospital where the majority of staff are Anglican and many of the patients long-stay, a Sung Eucharist might be held in the chapel. Many patients who are confined to bed miss the familiar words of the full Communion service, particularly the prayer of consecration, and when ambulant can join in the chapel service at a later celebration, either after Matins on a Sunday morning or at a suitably timed evening Communion when perhaps they might be accompanied by their families and friends after the regular visiting hours. A part-time chaplain should be able to arrange a weekly Holy Communion service in which there can be an offering up of the whole ethos of the hospital.

There is room for much experiment in hospital chapel services, with far more involvement in the whole liturgical

6

movement of the Church. There should be greater participation by both members of staff and patients; the service itself should speak far more effectively to the needs of the congregation. Language and symbolism should be simple yet meaningful and direct. The problems and fears, as well as the joys and thanksgivings, will form part of the offering in the ordinary services of the chapel and will also become a vital part of the whole liturgical worship of the hospital.

Regarding the admission to Holy Communion of members of other denominations who are not episcopally confirmed, the chaplain must be guided by the bishop and by the Acts of Convocations of Canterbury and York (XI, pp. 117f):

> Where a baptized communicant member of a church not in communion with our own is cut off by distance from the ministrations of his own church, he may be welcomed to communion by the incumbent. But if such person becomes an habitual communicant over a long period, the claims of the Church to full conformity with its requirements should be pressed upon his conscience.

RELAYED SERVICES

Where the services can be relayed from the hospital chapel it is helpful to announce at the beginning of the service a special greeting to the patients who are listening: "Good morning, everyone. This is the service from the hospital chapel being relayed to your bedside. We welcome you. . . ." Patients should be encouraged to participate as fully as possible, joining in the hymns and prayers whenever able, emphasizing thereby the corporate Christian fellowship and the sharing of the worship of the whole Church. Hymns should be announced and if the first line is read this will allow time for patients both in the congregation and in the ward to find the hymn in their books.

Such a relay system can also of course be used to broadcast morning and evening prayers.

OCCASIONAL OFFICES AND
SPECIAL SERVICES

Baptisms will not usually be performed in the hospital chapel, but on occasions when a request is received from a member of staff, who has perhaps served the hospital for many years, about the baptism of a child, exception can be made. This can be done of course only with the full permission of the family's parish priest.

Churchings should always take place in the parish church unless for some exceptional reason—e.g., the young mother has to remain in hospital for some little time after the birth of the baby. There will usually be much misunderstanding and superstition about both baptism and churching in the minds of many, and the chaplain can take this opportunity to teach and instruct, as well as to link up the family with their own parish.

Confirmation is not often administered in hospital, but when the occasion does arise, particularly amongst long-stay patients or those who are seriously ill, the diocesan bishop will come and confirm after the patient has been duly instructed. For members of staff suitable arrangements can be made at a neighbouring church after proper reference has been made both to the vicar of the church in question and to the nurse's parish priest. Where patients are ambulant the service might take place in the hospital chapel.

Memorial services: sometimes it will be necessary to hold a memorial service for a member of staff who has died after faithful service to the hospital and its community. Leaflets of the form of the memorial will normally be printed, a special lesson read by a member of staff, and a short address given perhaps by a colleague at the express wish of the family. Funeral services are not held in the chapel at all, but a special service might be arranged for the friends of one who has given his body to the hospital for purposes of medical research.

Special services might be held throughout Lent and Holy Week: for example there can be a weekly lunch-hour service (12.30–12.55 p.m.) with a special preacher or a particular theme discussed. A weekly intercessory service or bible reading can also be arranged when various aspects of the worldwide Church can be thought and prayed about by members of the staff.

Compline or informal evening prayers might be said together at the end of the day's work, and each chaplain can use his own discretion about the organization of staff Sunday services, St Luke's-tide services, etc. Services of nine lessons and carols will probably form an important part of the Christmas festivities and provide excellent opportunities for various members of the hospital staff to participate and read lessons.

Much will depend upon the particular circumstances of the local hospital, and each chaplain will adapt his programme accordingly.

5

The Chaplain's Ministry
on the Wards

When the chaplain comes to bring the Church's ministry to his
patients on the ward, his work brings him alongside that of the
doctor, not as an adversary, but as an ally. Once they were
both one and the same. Now they still do the same work, but
each from a different angle. Both are endeavouring, along with
many others, to restore the patient to health: to soundness of
body, mind, and spirit. This relationship has been described
in the following terms:

> Across the patient's bed we face each other; you in your white coat,
> a stethoscope in your hand; I in my black coat with a prayer book
> in my hand. At the beginning we were one, since the beginning we
> have always been together, unavoidably related, and when you are
> true to the oath of medicine and I true to the ordination vows, the
> centre of interest has been, is and must always be in the man on the
> bed, your patient, my parishioner, God's creation. And if we
> work in unity together, the patient will come to see, to know, to love
> the Father God who through us, in us, by us, and *in spite* of us, re-
> mains the ultimate one who . . . healeth all our diseases and for-
> giveth all our iniquities.[1]

BIBLE-READING

The more familiar both prayers and Bible readings are, the
more helpful they will be to sick patients, for in periods of

[1] R. K. Young and A. L. Meiburg, *Spiritual Therapy* (Hodder and
Stoughton, 1961) p. 171.

weakness any effort to think about something which is unfamiliar is apt to be a strain. It is here that the use of gospel
stories and selected psalms is so relevant and important. Many
patients will ask for a bible, and there should always be an
adequate supply on each ward of the hospital, while others are
made available at the back of the chapel. The chaplain will
help guide the patient to suitable passages of scripture, or will
himself read to those who are in pain or discomfort. It may be
useful to distribute small copies of the Gospels or to outline
suitable passages from them on the leaflet given to patients on
admission. The Bible Reading Fellowship series will provide a
useful plan for regular reading and meditation. There are
useful lists of helpful scripture passages or verses for reading in
The Priest's Vade Mecum, Ed. T. W. Crafer (S.P.C.K., 1945),
pp. 56f.; *St Raphael Prayer Book for the Sick* (S.P.C.K.), and at
the end of the Office of "The Visitation of the Sick" in the 1928
Prayer Book.

PRAYER

The priest's prayers. Before the chaplain can pray effectively
at the bedside he must be aware of the needs of the patient.
There can be no set formula or "technique"; neither can there
be any rules or regulations as to when to pray or not to pray.
The priest must not only be open and receptive to the promptings of the Holy Spirit, he must also be alert to the spiritual
state of the patient. To this end his prayer must have *direction*.
Before he prays, misunderstandings may have to be clarified
and difficulties resolved. Many will see prayer as having magical effects—a formula to dispel all doubts and fears and cause
pain to cease. Each time the chaplain must come where the
patient actually is. There is the danger of set prayers being
recited in a stereotyped form when they will bear little relevance to the needs and desires of the patient.

In many instances it will be more helpful to pray at the
bedside without having screens put round the patient's bed,
for this can often cause embarrassment and create undue stress.

When the priest prays he will be calm, confident, and relaxed. If he is too self-conscious, tense, and anxious he will only irritate and increase the already existing fears of the patient. The reply of one patient to the chaplain's request "Shall I say a prayer?", "Yes, certainly, if you think it will help you", should be a salutary lesson in this respect.

As well as direction, the prayers of the chaplain should have *outlook*. They must look beyond the immediate situation. Far too often prayers at the beside are too aimless, vague, and general, when they should be full of hope, faith, love. The Lord's Prayer, appropriate verses of scriptures, a psalm, a short extempore prayer, or a blessing all instil confidence and give spiritual strength and support. Suitable prayers and affirmations should be learnt by heart, for the use of books and booklets from which prayers are read is out of place at such times.

The patient's prayers. So much will depend upon the physical condition of the patient. If he is very ill he may be unable to express himself in prayer and the chaplain will pray for him; or he can be encouraged to use ejaculatory prayers. Intercessory prayers can be used by those who are able to respond physically, and they can be shown how such prayers can become a channel of grace for the whole hospital. This will save preoccupation with self and one's own physical condition. They will be helped to bring their own sufferings in union with their Lord's to be hallowed by his all-holy sufferings. Much anxiety and fear will be eased when a patient realizes how his prayers can be used in this way.

The people's prayers. Prayers for and with patients should always be rooted and grounded in the prayers of the parish. The prayerful hands of the chaplain will be borne up on the prayers of the faithful, and the faith and hope of the patient will be sustained and strengthened by the intercessions of his fellow-Christians. The importance of the prayer group in hospital and/or parish cannot be over-emphasized.

The ministry of the chaplain will then be set against the background of the work and worship of the church and form part of its whole prayer-stream. He will then pray not as an individual chaplain but as the voice of the Church. A hospital community should be prepared to intercede for its sick as conscientiously as it attends to its medicine and surgery.

WARD SERVICES

The advisability of holding ward services will largely depend upon local circumstances. It seems questionable whether the ward service has an essential place in the acute general hospital where the average stay is short. There will of course be many patients who will fully appreciate such services, while others will look upon them as a quite unnecessary intrusion into their privacy and be resentful and embarrassed. Where there is a relay system short services of prayers can be broadcast from the chapel to each bedside, and patients who wish to listen-in can participate.

There seems to be a clear need of ward services in geriatric wards, and in some psychiatric wards, where patients are fairly long-stay and unable to attend chapel services. As both these types of patients love to sing hymns, and provided it is not too tiring or exhausting, much can be achieved when such ward services are properly conducted. In both geriatric and psychiatric hospitals short addresses can have a planned sequence week by week. Should the provision of suitable music prove difficult, the use of tape-recordings is recommended.

Where ward services are held in other types of hospitals they should be brief, well planned, and carefully prepared, and some attempt should be made to meet the needs of the particular patients on the ward. No service (apart from those held in the hospitals mentioned above) should last more than eight to ten minutes. Whenever possible members of staff should be invited to participate and so a sense of corporate worship encouraged. The chaplain should see that the time allocated be convenient for ward routine, and he should strictly adhere to the times set. Hymn-books or prayer-cards with large clear print should be available, and a simple theme should permeate the service. Both hymns and scripture passages should be carefully selected and over-emotionalism avoided. Lay helpers, either from the parish or the hospital, can assist with the singing and generally lend support to the ward service.

HOLY BAPTISM

The chaplain, particularly if he serves in a children's hospital or one in which there is a large maternity unit, will frequently be called to administer Holy Baptism in cases of emergency, i.e. when an unbaptized child's life is in danger or when a major operation is anticipated. When the child is admitted to hospital the normal procedure is for the ward staff to inquire from the parents whether the child has been baptized. If no baptism has taken place they will be asked if they desire baptism, should any emergency arise. Where no emergency arises and the parents still wish for the child's baptism, they should be referred to their own parish priest on the discharge of the infant from hospital.

In every instance of emergency baptism the desire must be forthcoming from the parents, and it is always helpful for one or both to be present. This affords the chaplain opportunity to speak to them about the meaning and significance of Holy Baptism. They should be reminded of their responsibility to see that the child is received into the Church when it returns home. If circumstances do not allow the parents to be present, the chaplain can send them a suitable letter enclosing a baptismal card.[1]

There may be occasions when owing to urgency of the child's condition or the chaplain being non-resident there will not be

---

[1] It will be helpful for future reference if the parish in which the baptism has taken place is clearly stated: "The baptism has been registered in the parish of . . .".

REPORT OF EMERGENCY BAPTISM[1]
(WHEN ADMINISTERED BY A MEMBER OF THE STAFF)

To be given as soon as possible to the appropriate chaplain for purposes o fpastoral follow-up and registration.

Christian Denomination ....

Christian Names of person baptized..

Date of birth .... Date of Baptism...............................

Father's Christian names..

Mother's Christian names...

Surname ....

Mother's name before marriage..
(Requested for Roman Catholic chaplain)

Home address ....

Witness to baptism, if any...

This is to certify that I, having the intention of doing what the Church wishes, administered baptism to the above named person by pouring ordinary water upon the head and saying audibly at the same time "N., I baptize thee in the Name of the Father and of the Son and of the Holy Ghost".

Signed.................................. Date................................

Note:
If it is not possible to pour water on the head of the person to be baptized, it may be poured on the body near the head.

[1] As in use at Dudley Road Hospital, Birmingham 18.

sufficient time for a priest to be found. Members of the nursing staff should therefore be instructed and prepared to administer such an emergency baptism. (See rubrics in "The Ministration of Private Baptism of Children in Houses" in the 1928 Prayer Book.) Anyone, baptized or unbaptized, of any or no creed, can perform a valid baptism, but it would of course be desirable for a sister or nurse of the child's own denomination to officiate. Should such an occasion arise the necessary particulars for the baptismal register should be forthcoming and the chaplain informed as soon as possible.

It will be found useful to keep specimen forms outlining the required information on the ward, such as that shown opposite.

The Parochial Registers Act of 1812, §4, requires the chaplain to send a certificate of all baptisms performed in the hospital to the incumbent of the parish in which the hospital is situated for entry in the parish register. A Baptismal Register is also frequently kept in the hospital and deposited when completed either in the church chest of the parish or in the Muniment Room of the Diocese of the family concerned.

The parish priest will be informed immediately about the baptism, by the sending of an appropriate card:

From the Chaplain of .... Hospital

.... born ....
the child of Mr and Mrs...
was baptized on...
and entry was made in the Hospital Baptismal Register No.............
The parents have been asked to make arrangements with you for
.... to be "received into the Church". If the above address should not be in your parish I should be grateful if you would re-direct this communication.

Date...................... Signed...................................
Chaplain

Normally there will be a small portable font which is kept either in the chapel or in the maternity ward for emergency baptisms. It should be placed on a white linen cloth, with cross and candlesticks, on a trolley or table, and filled with tepid water. If the baptism is to take place in a premature unit it will not be advisable to light candles because of the vital supply of oxygen. The form of service will be that of "The Ministration of Private Baptism of Children in Houses" and should consist at the least of the Blessing of the water, the actual baptism, Lord's Prayer, the Thanksgiving, and the Grace. A spoon will be convenient for use, particularly when the child is in an incubator. The ward sister or some other representative of the staff should be present as a witness to the baptism of a new member of the Church. Their presence will also enable them to see what is required should they themselves be called upon to baptize in an emergency. After the baptism it is important to see that the water blessed at the service is poured "to earth" and not emptied down a sink. The necessary information for the baptismal register should be ready for the chaplain and, if the mother has been unable to attend the baptism, he will immediately visit her on the ward.

Should the child not live, the chaplain will be notified and will attempt to comfort and sustain the mother. The parish priest should be informed as soon as possible, so that he can visit the family and help in the arrangements of a Christian burial.

CONFIRMATION

In psychiatric hospitals or others in which there are long-stay patients the chaplain will be given opportunity to prepare both adults and children for the sacrament of Confirmation. There will probably be practical difficulties about the arrangement of convenient times for instruction classes. Preparation can either take place in the ward, in a conveniently situated room, or in the chapel. It is essential for the chaplain to keep in closest co-operation with the parish priest of the patient. Often it will be found necessary to give individual instruction, and although this will prove time-consuming, it will have the added advantage of adapting both the method and length of such instruction to the physical and spiritual state of the patient. Should he be transferred to another hospital, the confirmee will then be commended by the chaplain to his colleague with appropriate information about the stage of instruction reached, so that such preparation can be continued.

PENANCE

There can be many practical difficulties about hearing confessions in a hospital, the chief one being that of privacy. Screens should be brought around the bedside and this will be so normal an occurrence in a large ward that the procedure will go largely unobserved. It is also probably somewhat easier to have some noise going on rather than the whole ward to be held in an absolute silence. Should the patient be ambulant then he can either be taken along to the chapel or to a nearby side room of the ward.

With the very weak patient it will not always be possible for a formal act of confession to be made. In such circumstances the chaplain will use his discretion, realizing the place of vicarious faith and penitence; for the sacrament should not be withheld because a patient is too ill to fulfil the preliminary conditions. There will be a place for conditional absolution when a patient is seriously ill or infirm. In some instances the patient will be prepared to make only a general act of confession. If there is true repentance he will be assured of God's mercy and forgiveness, and the chaplain will pronounce absolution in the words used in the Holy Communion service. No one should be discouraged because they are unable to put their repentance into words.

Perhaps the best plan in such a case is to fall back upon the familiar forms provided by the prayer book and try to breathe into them the intensity of our individual sorrow for sin and our individual longing for forgiveness. One of the simplest ways of preparing for a special confession is to use some familiar words of confession with a fresh sincerity and a fuller trust in God's mercy. Only remember that, whatever method we use, we are obliged to confess our sins to God; for without confession there is no forgiveness.[1]

Penance also forms a necessary preparation and background for the sacraments of Holy Communion, Holy Unction, and the sacramental act of the Laying on of Hands.

Guilt plays a great part in many cases of mental illness, but the psychiatric hospital chaplain must be careful to distinguish between a psychopathic sense of guilt, which arises from psychological trouble, and a real sense of guilt. Absolution, coupled with spiritual counsel, is of much help to the mentally disturbed patient, and it must always be remembered that the primary value of confession is absolution and not merely "getting something off one's chest". Absolution by the priest makes up for the imperfection of the confession of the mentally ill patient. By the grace of God the priest can absolve the neurotic patient if he is as penitent as it is possible for him to be, although his penitence may apparently amount to very little.

HOLY COMMUNION

Before the sacrament is brought to the ward it is essential for the chaplain to visit each communicant patient on the afternoon or evening before their reception. This will be an opportunity to explain to them the exact form the service will take and to see that they have a card on which the service is printed. He will also help them prepare themselves, leading them to simple acts of faith and repentance. Many will value this private conversation; some may wish to make their confession.

Much misunderstanding still exists in the minds of a number of people that reception of Holy Communion in hospital is "an insurance for death" rather than "an assurance of life", and

[1] A. W. Hopkinson, *Comfort and Confidence* (A. R. Mowbray, 1927) p. 66.

every opportunity will be taken for teaching and instruction. Many will never have received their communion away from their parish church before, and may be rather shy, or anxious, or tense about its reception in a hospital ward. A clearly printed card with appropriate prayers of preparation and thanksgiving and a shortened form of the Holy Communion service is obtainable from S.P.C.K.[1] Such cards can be retained by the patient, but if constantly in use it is important for them to be kept clean and not heavily thumb-marked.

It is the custom in some hospitals for members of the ward staff to collect the names of communicants and then notify the chaplain. Such a procedure has advantages where a part-time chaplain has a large hospital or a group of scattered hospitals, and therefore finds it extremely difficult to see each patient frequently. It has, on the other hand, distinct disadvantages if left in the hands of uninstructed members of staff. Where it is practicable, the chaplain himself should be responsible, with the help and co-operation of sympathetic staff, for the compilation of lists of patients who wish to receive the sacrament. Another method is for a perforated slip to be attached to the leaflet distributed to patients on admission, on which they can signify their desire to receive Holy Communion while in hospital. The slip can then be collected by the Sister and given to the chaplain. It is essential for the ward sister and the patients to be informed of the time of the chaplain's arrival so that everything will be ready when he comes to the ward. Each chaplain will be able to devise his own method of communication, and the following illustration (p. 86) is meant only to serve as a practical guide.

Effective co-operation is essential, so that the administration of the sacraments in the wards is carried out with the least possible delay or disruption of ward routine.

Normally the chaplain will bring the reserved sacrament from either the hospital chapel or his own parish church, if he serves as part-time chaplain. It is of the greatest value to use

[1] Tract No. 3249; in large print, No. 3249A.

...., HOSPITAL

WARD COMMUNIONS

Ward..

Day.................................... Time........................a.m.

Name of Patient	Bed No.	Name of Patient	Bed No.

the reserved sacrament in hospital for some of the following reasons:

1. There may not be time to celebrate in order to give communion to a dying patient.

2. It is not always possible on the part of the chaplain or that of the ward staff to allow the time for a clinical celebration in any or all wards, and there may be many patients who would not wish to be present at such a celebration or to be silent during it.

3. Patients may be too weak to stand the length of service for a clinical celebration.

4. The chaplain will frequently have to give sick communions

at an hour earlier than that of the celebration in chapel, and at any time of day or night.

5. Nurses and others whose hours of work make it impossible for them to come to communion at normal times may be communicated from the reserved sacrament at times more convenient for them—such as before the meal before night duty.

6. In communicating from elements reserved at the open communion in church or hospital chapel, a sick person more obviously shares in the general communion and sacrifice of the whole Church.[1]

There are various methods of reservation which the chaplain may use. To administer in both kinds, with an intincted host, the elements will be kept in a double pyx (see illustration p. 89). Only a small quantity of wine will be placed in the pyx for there will normally be frequent movement if the chaplain has to climb stairs or use lifts to reach the wards. The host will be intincted at the bedside and placed directly into the mouth of the patient. This saves any risk of infection which might arise with an ordinary chalice used from patient to patient and ward to ward. It also facilitates administration should the patient be forced to lie flat in bed, e.g. orthopaedic cases. An added advantage is that the patient will continue to receive in two kinds, which is the normal practice. The words of administration will be

> The Body of our Lord Jesus Christ, which was given for thee, and his Blood, which was shed for thee, preserve thy body and soul unto everlasting life. Take this in remembrance that Christ died for thee, and feed on him in thy heart by faith with thanksgiving.

Should the host be intincted for reservation part of the priest's wafer is dipped in the chalice after the consecration of the elements and each wafer touched with a small spot of consecrated wine. It is advisable to leave the hosts to dry on

[1] See *A Priest's Work in Hospital*, Ed. J. C. Cox (S.P.C.K., 1955) p. 69.

7

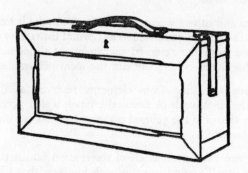

PORTABLE WARD ALTAR

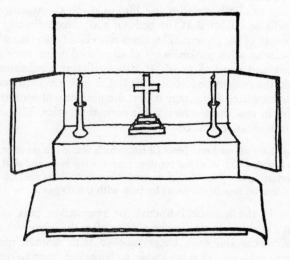

PREPARED FOR USE

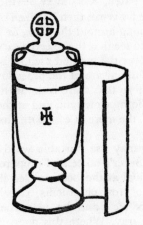

A DOUBLE PYX

INTINCTION OF THE HOST

the edge of the paten, for otherwise they will be apt to stick together. The hosts can then be taken out to the wards in an ordinary pyx hung around the neck, or in a ciborium.

The priest should see that the reserved sacrament is changed each week. Whatever the method used, it is essential that the patient be made fully aware of the procedure adopted by the respective chaplain so that there is the least possible strain or anxiety induced. Both beforehand and at the time of the Holy Communion itself, the more at ease both chaplain and patient can be the better.

Some hospitals may use portable ward altars which are normally kept in Sister's office and prepared in readiness for the chaplain's arrival at the bedside (see illustration p. 88). These will contain cross or crucifix, candlesticks, fair linen cloths, purificators etc., and be placed either on a small trolley, locker, or tray. Where this does not apply, a small altar together with accessories might be either left on the ward overnight or carried by the chaplain or a member of staff at the time of service.

It is always most helpful for patients who are to receive their communion to be grouped together as far as possible. Such groups should be so arranged that it is convenient for the chaplain to come alongside each patient in a reverent manner. The altar is set up in the middle for all to see and to join together in the service. If the chaplain has to move from one side of the ward to the other, the tray or trolley can be transferred with the help of an assistant. Apart from convenience, when patients are brought together it further instils the corporate nature of the sacrament and any sense of it being a "private communion" is completely lost. They are being united not only with their own parish church but with the whole Body of Christ.

If there is usually a large number of communicants it is of much help to the chaplain to have the assistance of a member of his congregation or perhaps preferably a sister or nurse who would be more familiar with ward routine and hospital procedure. The assistant can precede the chaplain and see that both ward and patients are ready for his arrival, as well as help with the cruets, etc., should a small communion set be used at the bedside.

The time of ward communions will be left to the arrangements in each local hospital. The whole-time chaplain will naturally be more able to divide the hospital into convenient sections and administer on various mornings of the week. He will also be able to see that a number of communicants can receive the sacrament on Sundays and Holy Days. The earlier he can be on the wards in the morning the better, so that a quiet atmosphere prevails, but he will be able to make the most suitable arrangements about time with the co-operation of the matron (or principal nursing officer) and the ward sisters. At whatever hour the chaplain comes, ward routine must continue, but as much silence and reverence should be observed as possible.

Some chaplains may wish to hold an "open" celebration in the middle of the ward, in view of all the patients, and to administer the sacrament to all those who are desirous of receiving. A portable altar can be wheeled in with all that is necessary for the service duly prepared. There is much to be said for such a practice in a geriatric hospital, or in a ward where there is not bound to be a continual round of activity and specialized nursing care. Such an "open" celebration would "let the communion be in common with the rest of the ward—this way the showing of religious activity would become less of an embarrassment, and people who never go to church would nevertheless know what happens in them".[1]

The form of the service when communion is administered from the reserved Sacrament will normally consist of: The Collect for Purity; Invitation; Confession; Absolution; Prayer of Humble Access (said together); Administration; Lord's Prayer (said together), and the Blessing. According to the physical state of the patient, the chaplain can use his discretion for the addition of Sursum Corda, Preface and Sanctus. When

---

[1] "Anglican Chaplain": Vol. 6, No. 19: June 1967, p. 22.

the Holy Communion is administered in "extreme necessity" the Prayer of Humble Access, Administration, Lord's Prayer, and Blessing only might be used.

It may sometimes be impossible for the patient to receive his communion owing to preparations for certain specialized treatments or tests. He may be in a sterile unit where it will sometimes prove most difficult for the sacrament to be brought in to him. In such instances he may be instructed in making a "spiritual communion", and leaflets might be printed with a suitable form of service.

Chaplains are on occasion told that the patient is unable to receive Holy Communion because he is "nil by mouth". This can occur sometimes before operations and prior to certain clinical tests being made. Quite recently the leading medical authorities of a London teaching hospital were consulted about this and it was reported that:

> they took great trouble to test the content of calcium in the communion wafers, and came to the conclusion that the small amount involved or possibly involved was miles outside the experimental error inevitable in the methods used for tests. They also thought that the harm done by denying patients Holy Communion would be much greater than any possible physical harm. Radiologists, anaesthetists, biochemists, physicians, and surgeons found general agreement that Holy Communion (considered as a physical matter only, of course) could have no adverse effect whatever on any biochemical test regularly performed, but that it should not be deliberately chosen on a day when a B.M.R. or glucose tolerance test was to be done.

> Instead, therefore, of the rule "Nothing by mouth after midnight" the Medical Committee decided that there was no need for patients to be dissuaded from taking Holy Communion before certain clinical procedures were carried out and laid down that no clinical, pathological, or operative procedure need debar a patient from receiving Holy Communion in the early morning, but that preferably it should not be administered on a day on which a B.M.R. or a glucose tolerance test has to be done. This ruling was circulated to all concerned in the hospital.[1]

[1] "Holy Communion in Hospital", "The St Raphael Quarterly", Vol. 7, No. 3, August 1964, p. 301.

THE LAYING ON OF HANDS

The laying on of hands can be administered according to the official form of service issued by the Convocations or, more frequently, in a less formal way. As it is a sacramental act there is no rigid form for its usage. By the resting of his hands on the person's head, the priest is bringing him in touch with that grace and power which has been made available in the Church by our Lord himself. The patient should be made as comfortable as possible and, whether the act is carried out formally or informally, the hands should be firmly laid upon the patient's head while prayers are said. There often ensues a deep sense of peace, calmness, and confidence.

It will be used far more frequently than Holy Unction, though it can also form part of that sacrament, being administered immediately prior to the act of anointing. Wherever possible the laying on of hands should be a corporate act, with a small group of intercessors present to uphold both priest and sufferer. This also prevents the act from becoming too "person-centred" and emphasizes the corporate concern of the Church, whose members share in their fellow-member's pain and suffering. The Church is working continuously in the hospital ward through its doctors, nurses, and students, and their participation and co-operation can help them to be more aware of their vocation as a healing fellowship, as members of the Body of Christ. *The Church is never just the chaplain at work.*

HOLY UNCTION

Whereas the laying on of hands can be frequently used, the sacrament of Holy Unction will be administered sparingly where there is serious illness, prior to an operation, or during a prolonged period of weakness. There is still much confusion about this sacrament of healing, for many link it with "Extreme Unction". Although it can be used *in extremis*, the origin of the term comes from the fact that anointing was the *last* in order of the many anointings (baptism, confirmation, ordination, coronation, and in serious illness) in the churches of Western Europe.

Very careful preparation is necessary, including acts of *faith*, *charity*, and *penitence*. The patient will be encouraged to place his whole trust and confidence in the will of God. The healing that ensures will not necessarily be physical, for Holy Unction is a ministry primarily to the soul.

The service, "The Administration of Holy Unction and the Laying on of Hands", is published by the authority of the Convocations of Canterbury and York by S.P.C.K. and A. R. Mowbray. A form is also published by the Guild of St Raphael. The oil used is pure olive oil consecrated by the bishop of the diocese, usually on Maundy Thursday, and made available to priests. If the need arises the priest himself can consecrate, using the following prayer:

> O Almighty Lord God, who hast taught us by thy Holy Apostle St James to anoint the sick with oil in thy name, and that the prayer of faith shall save him that is sick; bless this oil, we beseech thee, that whosoever shall be anointed therewith may be delivered from all troubles of body and mind, and from every assault of the powers of evil; through Jesus Christ our Lord. Amen.

The oil is kept in an oil-stock in either the aumbry or tabernacle, and it is preferable for it to be set apart from the reserved sacrament. When the sacrament is administered at the bedside a white cloth will be placed on the locker, together with a small glass containing some balls of cotton wool or breadcrumbs. The chaplain will begin by laying both hands on the patient's head and reciting the first part of the service. Next he dips the thumb of his right hand into the oil-stock and makes the sign of the cross on the patient's forehead. The oil is afterwards wiped with the cotton wool which is burned, and the chaplain cleanses his thumb and fingers with the lavabo and cotton wool. Holy Unction will normally be accompanied by the laying on of hands.

Should the patient have received Holy Unction or the laying on of hands from his parish priest before his admission to hospital, it will give added significance to close co-operation and to the importance of the Church's ministry of healing if besides informing the chaplain of this when commendation is made, the parish priest could also send a suitable note to the hospital doctor.[1]

From the Rev..

                         Date................................

Dear Sir/Madam,

        This is to inform you that Mr/Mrs............................

of.. who is one of my parishioners, has received the sacrament of Holy Unction and the laying on of hands prior to admission to hospital under your care, in accordance with the usage of the Church of England.

        I think you will like to know this.

                Yours faithfully,

                  ....

If the patient is able to come to the hospital chapel the sacrament can be administered in the setting of the Eucharist. Just before the blessing he will come to the altar rail and kneel while the chaplain recites the opening words from the Gospel. After the laying on of hands and the anointing the patient is led by the right hand and raised up to return to the congregation before the eucharistic blessing is given.

When the patient is *in extremis* Holy Unction will precede the Viaticum.

As preparation is important so is the subsequent pastoral care. The patient will be visited by the chaplain soon after, when there has been a period of quiet and peace, and be

[1] See "The St Raphael Quarterly", Vol. 3, No. 3 August 1959, p. 84.

helped to sustain hope and strengthen faith with acts of thanksgiving, prayer, and intercession. There will be a joyful expectant confidence that God's love is working within the patient for his wholeness. Should the patient be gradually restored to total health he can be led to give thanks and offer his renewed strength for more effective service to Almighty God and his Church. If there is no outward sign of physical improvement or alleviation of pain the sufferer can be taught to offer his pain in union with that of his Lord's afflictions. He can be shown that sometimes healing comes gradually or in an indirect way. If he has been given adequate preparation he will not be disappointed if there is no physical healing, for one thing will be certain—there will always be a deep sense of joy peace, and utter resignation to the will of God. God has been at work, although for the present his purpose may not be clear or his will revealed. The *victim* will have become the *victor*.

6

The Chaplain's Ministry to the Mentally Ill

The reader will already be familiar with the prevalence of mental illness. Various mental disorders are among the greatest causes of long-term incapacity, and about half the beds provided by the Health Service are occupied by psychiatric patients. One man in fourteen and one woman in nine can expect to be admitted to a psychiatric hospital at least once in their lifetime. The problem itself is of course much greater than mere figures.

THE PICTURE

Since the 1959 Mental Health Act a whole revolution of change has taken place in the attitude towards the mentally ill. Psychiatric hospitals may still be very much out-dated architecturally, but within old buildings miracles of curative power are being performed. Half of these large and ungainly hospitals were built before 1870 and are still overcrowded, but much if not all of their custodial care has now disappeared. From places of detention they have become ante-rooms to health. Thanks to modern drugs and the concept of the therapeutic community these barrack-like structures have come to serve an entirely different function. Short-term medical and psychological treatment means that nine out of ten patients are discharged within a year, a great number of them after a few weeks. Psychiatric hospitals are now closely linked with out-patient clinics and day hospitals where there is much scope for team-work, not only with the patients themselves but, equally important, with their families, in understanding some of their problems and difficulties.

By far the greater number of patients now enter hospital quite voluntarily and admission has been brought into line with that of general hospitals. Where compulsory admission is necessary, then either the patient's next-of-kin or a mental welfare officer can sign such an application. Under normal circumstances the signatures of two doctors (one of whom will be a psychiatrist) would be necessary, and a period of twenty-eight days for observation would be required. When the admission is an emergency, one medical signature would be needed and a "three day order" would detain the patient. The majority of psychiatric hospitals are now "open", with a small minority of locked wards, for only a very small number of psychiatric patients need security precautions.

THE THERAPEUTIC COMMUNITY

Another sign of progress has been the breaking down of an authoritative structure and the establishment of a therapeutic community within the hospital. There are now far more informal lines of communication, and group meetings (in which patients are encouraged to speak freely and frankly) form an important part of treatment. Much of the rigid hierarchy has fortunately disappeared, for the old institutional process was proved anti-therapeutic, and as a result of long-stay in hospital patients were submitted to a secondary disease which has come to be known as "institutional neurosis". These days patients are more and more drawn into active participation in both treatment and the routine and welfare of the ward. Such group meetings are generally unstructured, and patients and staff communicate and interact as informally as possible. Indignation, anger, resentment, can be brought out into the open and be accepted and worked through in a supportive environment. Into such free communication are brought psycho-dynamic insights in order that assessments and interpretations might be made to patients. In this way they are able to become more and more aware of what is happening in their own individual lives, and such understanding becomes therapeutic in itself. Dr Denis Martin of Claybury Hospital has written:

> To feel accepted, though unacceptable, is of the very essence of the therapeutic process, leading in time to a self-acceptance which paradoxically transforms the individual more or less. . . . To express rage, in spite of the terrifying fantasies, in the presence of the object of rage, is a profoundly reassuring experience, leading ultimately to the dissipation of infantile rage and its replacement by normal assertiveness and anger. Important in this whole process is the help and support patients can give to one another.[1]

VARIOUS TYPES OF MENTAL DISORDERS

THE NEUROSES

Mental illness is most difficult to define in concise terms and the various types are merely useful designations for various classifications. The most common of the psychoneurotic disorders is *anxiety*. The patient is usually very restless, easily irritated and depressed. Physical expressions of anxiety are palpitation, headaches, nausea, and pressure round the head. The anxiety-ridden person is liable to panic states, usually with conditioned phobias. Pure anxiety often occurs where there is no apparent strain or stress inducing it.

Depression can either be *reactive* (a response to stress of some kind) or *endogenous* (an unexplained constitutional reaction). There will often be tiredness, indigestion, or some physical symptom. A loss of interest in usual pursuits will be marked, and slowness in action and thought may give way to weeping and difficulty in concentrating. Home duties become neglected and appearance unkempt. The early hours of the morning seem the worst part of the day. There are feelings of great unworthiness and/or guilt. In severe depression there will always be the risk of suicide. The depressed patient may have

---

[1] Denis Martin, *The Role of Religion in Mental Health* (N.A.M.H., 1967) p. 11.

self-reproaches about sexual misdemeanours, or self-accusations about having committed crimes of violence.

The second group are the *phobic reactions*. The anxiety or fear is related in an unrealistic and often quite exaggerated form to specific objects, situations, or events. The various phobias include fear of open spaces, enclosed spaces, crowds, etc.

Obsessive-compulsive neuroses are characterized by the obsessional occurrence of intruding ideas, images, and thoughts. The patient has an irresistible urge to repeat certain acts which he knows to be abnormal and absurd but over which he has very little control, e.g. washing his hands repeatedly, taking hours to dress himself, indulging in various rituals and monotonous repetitions. Such behaviour and preoccupation makes life almost unbearable.

It is important to state that in *conversion hysteria* the mechanisms of "flight into illness" etc. are not usually conscious motivations, and it is important therefore to distinguish between the hysteric and the malingerer. Careful assessment and extreme discretion are most necessary in exercising pastoral care. There is usually a loss of some physical function without the usual evidence of physical disease: paralysis, blindness, fits and faints, etc., which prevent the patient from having to face up to some difficult or disagreeable situation. They also often provide a secondary means of gaining sympathy and attention.

In recent years there has arisen another category which has many features in common with the neuroses—*psychomatic disorders*. Here there is organic illness with the accompanying physiological changes, but it is one in which psychological factors seem to have initiated the disease process. Long continued tensions, worries, and strains produce damage to bodily tissue. The most frequently occurring are various skin complaints, abdominal troubles, sinusitis, asthma, etc.

THE PSYCHOSES

There are two main groups—*organic* and *functional*. *Organic* psychoses are those resulting from known changes in the brain such as injury, tumours, infections. In this category too would come the psychoses associated with old age, through arterial disease or degeneration. Most common are the *functional* psychoses, where no change can be detected in the brain tissue, structure or metabolism. Much research is at present being carried out as to their cause.

Unlike the patient suffering from a neurosis, the psychotic sufferer has very little insight into his condition. He does not know he is ill and so will not accept the fact; hence he lives in a world of unreality, though at the same time it has much reality for him.

Schizophrenia.   The most common of the psychotic disorders is that of *schizophrenia*, in which there is almost complete loss of contact with the outside world, and regression to rather primitive elements in the emotional life. The patient neglects everyday habits, and does not bother to wash or take interest in his personal appearance. There is a lack of affection and emotional response. The disorder often manifests itself in the form of occasional outbursts of disturbed and destructive behaviour. Very little is known about its origin and its progress is somewhat unpredictable. Among its characteristics is a severe disruption of thinking, feeling, and behaviour. Conversation is intermingled with much irrational content, and patients are inclined to talk for hours on end on religious and philosophical subjects or in psuedo-scientific jargon. Even new words, expressions, and illogical word-formations will be introduced.

Of particular concern to the chaplain will be the conception of sin and guilt, and thoughts that prompt the patient to feel in touch with the Holy Spirit, or think he is God himself.

Four varieties of schizophrenia are recognized:

(a) *Hebephrenic.* There will be disorder of mood and thought, and bizarre hallucinations and delusions. The thought processes become autistic and the patient is inclined to have suspicious and hostile moods.

(b) *Catatonic.* Here there will be disorder of mood, thought, and behaviour, resulting in a very withdrawn state. The patient may stand immobile for hours on end, quite unrespon-sive although consciousness may be clear.

(c) *Simple schizophrenia.* A disorder of mood only and far more uncommon than the above. Some of the clinical features are different and there will be no hallucination or delusions.

(d) *Paranoid.* In this form of schizophrenia there will be dis-order of mood, thought, behaviour, and of contact with reality. It develops more in later life. There are grandiose ideas and delusions and hallucinations are present.

Manic-depression. The patient experiences recurrent attacks of depression and elation. The depression will be acute and crip-pling, and there will be self-accusatory delusions—he imagines he has committed most serious crimes and sins and that there is no hope at all for him. Auditory hallucinations will prompt him to imagine that people are talking to and about him, through radio, television, etc. Consequently he will become dejected, anti-social, and agitated. A suicide tendency will have to be watched.

During the manic state the mood swings to elation and hypomania. The patient will often be seen to write most lengthy and incoherent letters, particularly to the most prom-inent personalities. His grandiose ideas and elation are apt to affect both insight and judgement.

Paranoid disorders. The patient will have delusions in which he is the victim of persecution. People are constantly plotting against him and he is convinced that there are schemes to destroy him or poison him.

Involutional psychosis. This disorder occurs in men aged about 50–65 and in women from 40–55. The symptoms are fatigue, pressure in the head, loss of interest, feelings of inadequacy, drastic and sudden change in behaviour and habits. Severe agitated depression will also be present. There are delusions of hypochondriacal type and ideas of unworthiness and guilt. Delusions also take the form of deprivation—no money, no family, no friends. Hallucinations occur and there is the risk of suicide.

VARIOUS TYPES OF TREATMENT

There are two main approaches to the treatment of the mentally ill: the *physical treatments* such as electro-convulsive therapy, deep or modified insulin therapy, narcosis, leucotomy, deconditioning, hypnosis, and chemotherapy (tranquillizers, antidepressants, sedatives, abreactive drugs, etc.), and the *psychotherapeutic treatments* which include analytically orientated methods, individual or group psychotherapy, counselling, etc.

The whole concept of rehabilitation has been more and more developed over recent years, and there is at present a strong movement towards "industrial therapy". Patients who work in the factory within the hospital receive the normal rate of pay for the job done, and so are provided with an incentive for improvement which perhaps was missing from the former concept of occupational therapy. Earnings are calculated separately for individual patients, and such a system has proved most successful, not only in combating both idleness and apathy, but also in restoring the patient's sense of usefulness and creativity. Often sufficient progress is achieved to enable the patient to participate in normal work outside.

As well as the resumption of work, rehabilitation aims at leading to a return to normal social involvement in the community. Hostels, lodgings, and half-way houses are gradual but important steps back into modern urban life, with more and more responsibility being gained. Links with the community are being increasingly established and the care of the mentally ill now involves more general practitioners, general hospitals, and public health services, as well as the psychiatric hospital itself.

THE MENTALLY SUBNORMAL

The Mental Health Act, 1959, defined subnormality as "a state of arrested or incomplete development of mind (not

8

amounting to severe abnormality) which includes subnormality of intelligence and is of a nature or degree which requires
or is susceptible to medical treatment or other special care or
training of the patient". Severe subnormality is defined as "a
state of arrested or incomplete development of mind which
includes subnormality of intelligence and is of such a nature or
degree that the patient is incapable of living an independent
life or guarding himself against exploitation, or would be so
incapable when of an age to do so" (Section IV).

As will be clear from the above definitions there is an important difference between the mentally ill and the mentally
subnormal. In the former circumstances there has been only a
temporary disturbance in the patient's normal mental functioning. In the latter such a normal functioning has never
existed.

Much research is at present being developed in the whole
sphere of mental subnormality and in discovering possibilities
of prevention, alleviation, education, and training. The chaplain will have a twofold ministry, directed both towards the
parents of the mentally subnormal and the patients themselves.

Many major difficulties confront the family and they will
be in need of both psychological and spiritual support. On
account of the parents' deep emotional involvement and feelings of guilt, disappointment, and underlying frustration, the
chaplain's ministry will be an essential factor in an intellectual
and emotional acceptance of their overall problems. He must
first help them to *accept themselves* as parents without feelings of
guilt or social stigma, and then assist them to *accept their mentally subnormal children*. Some may want to deny the reality and
refuse to believe that this could possibly happen to them.
Others may indulge in wishful thinking and hope that some
miraculous cure might be found to restore normality. One of
the most important of the chaplain's works will be to help the
parents face up realistically to the situation and accept the
child as a worthwhile human being to be loved and nurtured.

Guilt feelings can lead to over-pampering, over-indulgence,
and over-protection of the child This will only tend to inhibit

the development of his potentialities towards independence. Problems also develop over other children of the family, and the relationships between the mentally subnormal child and other siblings has to be carefully watched. Complicated issues arise over the question of keeping the child at home or placing him under care in hospital. Educational procedure and other activities have to be worked out in the family.

The parish priest or whole-time chaplain must be especially understanding, sensitive, and sympathetic, for skill and patience will be required in all his aspects of pastoral care of families of the mentally subnormal.

At the outset the chaplain ministering in a hospital for the mentally subnormal must be fully aware that in dealing with the patients he is not caring for a "different" kind of person. The patients are fundamentally the same as so-called normal people, only they live with a background of lower levels of intelligence, and what differences there appear to be are quantitative rather than qualitative. Unless the chaplain sees this he will not be able to effect any kind of meaningful personal relationship which is so essential to his ministry.

Some characteristics of the mentally subnormal patient are important for him to observe, for an infinite amount of time and patience will be required in his ministry to them. He will generally find that they are slow to learn and to grasp any new situation. Many of them will also lack insight and judgement, with a complete lack of understanding of their needs. Their ideas about God are closely related to ideas and feelings they have to other people about them. So much will naturally be dependent upon what religious upbringing they have had, the limitations which their handicap imposed upon them, and what relationships they have had with other people. The chaplain might be able to bear witness to the nature of God, communicated in such a way that they have as clear and true a picture as possible—one who loves them and does not reject them when they are naughty, for many will seem to feel they have been punished or are deserving of punishment.

A lack of worth or responsibility are other factors in their minds which will influence the chaplain's approach to them. He will therefore seek to enhance their sense of worth and discourage feelings of inferiority. Again, a sense of responsibility will be instilled when patients become so completely satisfied with their dependence that they are happy with a merely passive existence. In his personal contacts he will lead them to a genuine concern for others when they become aggressive or hostile. He will also help them understand, accept, and work through their bouts of anger. Only as they feel themselves to be loved can they offer love to others.

The chaplain will often meet with disappointments, but he will soon impair any relationships he has managed to build up if he makes evident any signs of discouragement or impatience. Always must he emphasize the positive elements of love, forgiveness, faith, and hope. Mentally subnormal patients are most susceptible to atmosphere, and they soon sense whether those about them care for them or not. The chaplain who is prepared to offer companionship and a deep sharing of their problems and difficulties will find that he has much to learn from his patients.

The symbolic acts of Christian worship mean much to those who are retarded, for they can do much to convey a sense of divine love and acceptance. To prepare his patients for confirmation is no easy task for the priest. He will rely on his discretion for many will be deemed unsuitable, yet selection can be a most exacting task. There will be many who will be inarticulate and "he should look for devotion and love for our Lord rather than for much intellectual acceptance of doctrine, though he should be satisfied that the candidate knows that he needs God's help and what God does for him in the sacraments".[1] At the altar Holy Communion should be administered by intinction to avoid any misuse of the sacred elements. The addresses given in the hospital chapel should be short, simple,

---

[1] *A Priest's Work in Hospital*, Ed. Cox (S.P.C.K., 1955) p. 153. See also *Number Unknown* (C.I.O., 1965) Appendix 3, "The Work of the Hospital Chaplain", and the outline of a confirmation course for the mentally subnormal, p. 77.

and direct, well illustrated with appropriate stories and perhaps visual aids. Prayer and meditation have effect on the deeper level of their minds, and properly conducted meditations and periods of silence can free them from negative and depressing thoughts, as well as bring home to them the fact of the love and forgiveness of God.

The answer to many of the difficulties outlined above will lie in that peace within the chaplain himself which comes from God. When the mentally subnormal feel and see in him God's love and peace then there can be no limit to the hope given in the midst of their isolation, loneliness, and despair. The chaplain himself must be aware of a deep sense of vocation and mission, testifying at all times to the fact of God's over-ruling power and love. He will not be too concerned or worried about what practical limitations may seem to inhibit his ministry, for when he feels his own inability the Holy Spirit is most operative.

THE ROLE OF THE CHAPLAIN IN THE PSYCHIATRIC HOSPITAL

Admission to a psychiatric hospital can be a frightening experience for someone who is already fearful and anxious. It will be one of the initial tasks of the chaplain to break down many of the misconceptions which the newly admitted patient might have about the hospital and its treatment, and explain away many of the alarming fantasies which might have been built up.

Obviously much of what has already been observed earlier about ministering in a general hospital will also apply to the chaplain's task in a psychiatric hospital, and some differences in his ministry have already been outlined. There are various features, however, of his work which will demand special attention.

It is quite imperative that he has a thorough understanding of some of the more common mental disorders and their treatments. Fortunately much is being done in this field these days by lectures in theological colleges, theological students spending periods of training in psychiatric hospitals, seminars and visits during post-ordination training, clinical theology, and field groups of the Institute of Religion and Medicine, etc. A psychiatric hospital is not merely a place where mentally ill people come to be looked after. It is a community, and the chaplain's contribution to this community sense is all important and his ability to work as a member of the therapeutic team must be clearly in evidence. His whole concept of his particular role is of vital import not only to himself but also to all those amongst whom he ministers. If he has been adequately trained he will have much to contribute, and although it is important to remember that

> a great deal of stress is often laid on the fact that the priest ought not to be a psychiatrist . . . in so far as he is trying to alter human personality, then his aims have many similarities. One hopes that the new techniques being discovered in psychotherapy may enable the minister to be more effective in his dealings with people.[1]

He will see the patient as a person to be loved, and will minister to him, along with others, in the totality of his being, and in his relationships with others. Often the mentally sick patient will have lost his ability to form creative relationships, for the deprivation of emotional security in childhood has probably been one of the basic causes of his present disorder. He will accept the patient as he is, and his effectiveness as a psychiatric hospital chaplain will often depend on his ability to relate as a person, for the good news of the gospel can never be relayed through an image but only through a person. He will endeavour to identify himself with the patient as far as is possible, seeing his weakness as part of his own, his helplessness as evidence of his own utter inadequacy, his cry for help as re-echoing his own need of God's grace and forgiveness.

His ability to *listen* and to come face to face with the real person will mean much—to see behind the torment created by the disorder a human being who is a child of God. He should

[1] "Contact" No. 11: "Pastoral Encounter", June 1964, p. 9.

not be over-submissive; neither must he be superior, but patient and tolerant. Besides having an adequate knowledge of some of the irrational behaviour displayed by his patient, he will also need to understand himself, his own fears and failings, facing these honestly in himself before he comes to others.

Pastoral skill will be needed to distinguish between what the mentally sick patient *wants* and what he really *needs*, and never to confuse the two issues. In his tolerance he will not be weak; in his permissiveness he will not succumb or evade. Neither must he be held captive to the many subtle demands of the patient. His pastoral care should seldom be seen in isolation but always as an integral part of the psychiatric team.

With the acutely psychotic patient there may be very little he can do from the human standpoint, but in his very presence —his "being there"—the chaplain communicates that he cares, he accepts, he loves. He will have an important part to play as treatment progresses, encouraging, supporting, and establishing relationships. Just as the whole manner and attitude of the psychiatrist—the "person"—is all important, so too is it equally imperative for the priest's approach to be natural, with a firmness mingled with flexibility, an authority which is quiet and dignified. He will participate in group meetings but in his eagerness to be absorbed into the team he will be careful not to lose his own identity as priest and pastor. If he pretends to be other than what he really is; if he is more secure adopting another role; if he is so threatened that he has to use other language than his own, then his position as chaplain will be much in question.

Sometimes he will have to be content and wait for psychiatric treatments to have their effect, for the timing element of pastoral care is most important. After treatment, issues usually become clearer as life begins to take on new perspectives. When a truer sense of need and sin is developed then the chaplain can help each individual patient's growth in love and trust, and perhaps restore him to a sacramental life which has lapsed, and to prayer where it has been neglected. He can begin to meet the fundamental needs of the patient in a far more effective way than if he had attempted to help when the insight of the patient was still distorted and reasoning and reassurance proved futile and meaningless. With understanding and much patience he will help the patient re-establish himself in the worshipping life of the Church.

Many patients will have strong religious convictions and will attend the chapel services regularly, although a large number now go home for weekends. Services should be made as attractive as possible and special occasions are much appreciated, e.g., Harvest Thanksgiving services, Carols, etc. The singing of hymns will normally be hearty and where the selection has been wise and discreet such singing can have much therapeutic effect.

There is no stronger antidote to anxiety and fear than the reception of the sacrament of Holy Communion, where the broken mind of the patient can be offered up in union with the broken body of our Lord, and the peace which passes all understanding become part of himself. Many will be unable to express themselves, and be "quite inaccessible religiously, and some may be unfit to take part in the Eucharist, but if the life of those who care for them is rooted there, it reaches them through those unconscious relationships which, like children, they can enter into".[1] In the sacramental approach of the ministry of healing the mentally ill can find direction and purpose for much of their meaninglessness and futility, faith for the fear which constantly torments them, and reconciliation for the estrangement which they so clearly experience.

COMMUNITY CARE

It will be an important function of the chaplain's ministry to *teach* and *interpret* to members of the community the part they can play in forming a real link between the psychiatric hospital and society at large. Not so long ago such hospitals were enclosed structures and high walls were erected, not so much to keep the patients in as to shut the public out. They had farms

[1] *Religion and Mental Health*, N.A.M.H., 1960, p. 12.

and workshops and were completely self-contained communities. Fortunately such a conception has now completely disappeared. More and more channels with the community are opening up. Mental illness is now seen as one of the country's greatest *social* problems. A recent slogan for a "Mental Health Year" showed to the public that it was "Everybody's Business".

The mentally ill need all the help the community can muster. There is still too much prejudice and hostility, apathy and fear. In what is to many an entirely unfamiliar world, the need for an outstretched hand of acceptance is paramount. The Church has still much to learn before it can adequately meet the challenge of "after-care". Members of local congregations can, if they will, represent to the discharged psychiatric hospital patient the continuing love and care of God and his people, but, as Dr Denis Martin reminds us,

> When one looks at the average church community alongside our experience of the kind of community that has proved therapeutic, the thing that stands out is the stultifying and repressive effect of Christian respectability. Conventional and superficial good behaviour is much safer than a dynamic spirit of love and acceptance, and this is what the church community implicitly demands most frequently. . . . The common conception of Christian love is a superficial kindness based upon the suppression of bad feeling with gossip and umbrage-taking as the frequent and destructive outlet. This kind of goodness can only be achieved at the cost of severe inner conflict. . . . The relativity of the behaviour pattern which is acceptable is shown by the way it varies from one denomination to another, and from one Church to another. In this kind of community it is almost impossible to be a real person and to live through experiences of emotional sincerity.[1]

PASTORAL CARE OF THE FAMILY

The attitude of members of the family to the mentally sick patient often plays a large part in the care of the patient for good or ill. If they can be shown that he is unwell then they

---

[1] *The Role of Religion in Mental Health*, N.A.M.H., 1967, p. 14.

lose much of their exasperation and anguish. It is his mental disorder that causes him to appear other than himself, to be unreasonable perhaps, or unapproachable. Unfortunately many families will feel ashamed at a son or daughter who is in a psychiatric hospital and will not allow anyone to know, and so the patient will return to a deeper state of isolation and "apart-ness". Some other families will think up all sorts of things to tell people in order to prevent them from knowing John has been "put away". It is a sad reflection but conditions at home can sometimes cause and aggravate mental ill-health. On the other hand, the best of home environment and all the devotion shown are no substitutes for psychiatric hospital facilities once the patient becomes acutely mentally disturbed. Indeed, there can be the hidden danger of too much love in the home, too much devotion for the person's emotional stability.

Families should be encouraged to welcome the patient back home for weekends, to be interested in him, to be understanding towards him, to show him he is still an accepted member of the family, and in a very real sense to see themselves as partners with the staff of the local hospital in restoring the patient gradually back to health and wholeness. Each visit home will have to be handled differently, and the full co-operation between his family and hospital is essential. Families can be shown how helpful it is to re-arrange some of the home routine if necessary so that the change from hospital to home does not prove too disrupting and disturbing. Normally the sooner he resumes his normal place in the home the better, and he can be helped to cultivate his former interests and hobbies.

PRIEST AND PSYCHIATRIST

The gap is being gradually bridged between the two professions, but until the role of the priest in psychiatry is better defined and more specifically understood many of the pockets of resistance will remain. Chaplains and parochial clergy are now being asked to participate more and more in psychiatric areas. This is an exciting challenge, and it is the priest's duty to respond as adequately and fully as he can, offering his special skills and his unique message in order to bring peace and comfort to minds tormented.

At present the greatest need seems to be that of effective communication. Differences between priest and psychiatrist are very real and therefore it is essential that clarification and not confusion emerges. There is much overlap, but the dividing line is no "iron curtain", and true co-operation will be the unifying of two complementary approaches rather than any attempt to subordinate the one to the other. A recent writer sums up the challenge thus:

> The unique contribution of Christianity to the subject [psychiatry] is its ability to see in man, over and above his limitations and disturbances, the image of God, and to apply the indefinable but unique contribution of love. No other branch of medicine creates such a vast need for this and none has received such a meagre contribution from the Christian community. We are living at a time in the history of mankind when a unique opportunity is being offered to make amends. It will be a great pity if we neglect it.[1]

[1] J. Dominian, *Christianity and Psychiatry* (Faith and Fact Book, Burns and Oates, 1962) p. 135.

7

The Chaplain and his Training

If the ministry of the chaplain in hospital, whether it is part-time or whole-time, is to be really effective, and if it is to have any significant meaning for all concerned, then the chaplain must have adequate training and preparation. If he cannot unobtrusively demonstrate his effectiveness he has no right to be chaplain. Pastoral experience in the parochial setting will of course provide him with a most necessary background, but he needs more than this. There should be more involved than a mere "switch-over" from parish to hospital. If he is to take his place among other professional members of staff in the hospital he must have something constructive to contribute, for he should be looked upon as a colleague and not as a well-meaning amateur.

The obvious centre for such training will be a hospital—the clinical environment in which he hopes to serve as chaplain. In such a setting he will be confronted by tragedy and triumph, despair and faith, and will learn from "living human documents" (Boisen) what he cannot possibly learn merely from lectures or seminars. Face to face with those living situations which are apt to bring to light some of the inadequacies of his rational answers, he will be compelled to question both his theology and himself. Such "clinical" experience is not readily accessible outside such a setting as either a general or a psychiatric hospital, where clinical material can be written up, worked through, and studied together. Here too will come contributions from the various disciplines to the study of people and human relationships. The various crisis situations which will be met add depth to such an experience. It is

"clinical" because in training the priest will work under
supervision and so learn from his mistakes with the least
possible danger to both himself and the patients whom he
serves.

There will be added advantage if he is able to reside in the
hospital throughout the clinical training programme. He will
be able to sense the atmosphere of a hospital, and become a
part of its community, sharing its life and work with other
professions, and discussing together its problems and mutual
concerns. This interchange of experience will prove one of the
important features of his training, particularly if he is shown
how to examine them in their deepest implications of *involvement* and *commitment*.

Clinical training focuses on people, and not only will this
exposure to their various emotional and spiritual needs lead
the priest to a sense of the magnitude and gravity of his chaplaincy ministry, but it will also prompt him to a deeper
knowledge and understanding of himself. The programme
will be seen as something more intellectual and profound
than an opportunity to accumulate data or to compile useful
"do's" and "don'ts"—helpful as these may be in their proper
context. Pastoral skills are not enough in themselves, for they
cannot be effectively used until there has first been a thorough
understanding of the precise role of the priest or minister
in serving the sick in a secular society. The exact goals
of his ministry, the effectiveness of his work, the meaning
of his relationships, to the patient, to the staff and to himself
will have to be examined. Far more important than any
"technique" are his approach and his attitude, for he must
have not only the right training but also the right temperament.

Without training the hospital chaplain's approach can so
easily become irrelevant to the needs of his people—both
"healthy" and "sick". His theology must have adequate
answers for some of the questions men are asking. Unless the
chaplain understands his relationships with others, particularly
with those which make him feel anxious, threatened, and

insecure, he will spend a great deal of his time defending and protecting himself rather than helping and supporting others. In such a maelstrom of relationships which make up the modern hospital he must first be aware of himself as a person and must learn never to take himself for granted. He must know his weaknesses and deficiencies as well as his strengths and capabilities, so that the former might be rectified and the latter recognized and developed.

In an integrated programme of both theory and practice, individually supervised by an experienced chaplain who has the full support and co-operation of a medical and departmental staff, who are prepared to participate in the training, some of the fundamental questions which need to be asked are:

1. *How the staff function: Who are they?*

No chaplain can take up a chaplaincy appointment in such a specialized setting until he knows how it works, and what makes it tick. Certain facets of the health service and where it has application to his respective ministry must be familiar to him. An essential part of his training will consist in learning how to co-operate with others; to learn some of their language so that a meaningful dialogue can take place. (It is equally important, of course, for them to become familiar with his.) Both must be aware of the approach and the skill of the other; each must know where he is and why he is there. The strains and stresses facing hospital personnel must be clear to him so that his presence does not add to existing difficulties and anxieties or jar in those situations. In the inter-disciplinary relationship he will search for his own identity.

He will not substitute his newly discovered scientific data for his own pastoral approach; rather he will see it as something to be absorbed in the context of religious thought and discussion. It will be for him to remain aware of the ultimate concerns of a power that not only completes them but also transcends them.

2. *How the patient functions: Who are you?*

In the hospital situation the very nature and destiny of man will confront the chaplain; the "raw stuff of human existence" will thrust itself upon him.

After understanding the hospital, the student's next objective is to understand the most important person within it—the patient. What are some of the major factors in human personality? What are some of the causes of breakdown? What part does psychic conflict play in physical disease? He will need to understand some of the dynamics of human development and the emotional factors evident in illness. The "inner world" of the patient will be one of his chief areas of exploration, as the priest endeavours to sense the agony of self-despair, the anguish of apprehension and fear, and the acuteness of pain and suffering. Here too, relationships will be all important—the dynamics of person-to-person relationships. Sick people are apt to express feelings and emotions which they would not bring out under normal circumstances, and the chaplain will need to examine his whole pastoral dialogue. What meaning will his presence convey? What will his words express?

Such questions cannot be studied apart from the basic Christian doctrines of God, man, sin and salvation, and the whole theology of sickness and suffering. The chaplain cannot be of help until he understands the use and meaning of such theological concepts in human experience.

Again, the patient must not be seen in isolation, for he is no individual but part of a community. In that community he became sick and in that community he hopes to get well. At present he is isolated, fragmented, away from his normal community, and placed in an abnormal community which is in itself departmentalized and broken. This brokenness of human existence will need be an essential component of religious concern, for it will not be confined to the physical or the emotional alone but reach out to include the spiritual. The broken body impinges on the dimension of the broken mind with its inevitable distorted relationships. Infusing both will be the broken meaning of life itself. Healing must therefore take place on all levels of the patient's personality.

3. How the Chaplain functions: Who am I?

"Physician, heal thyself!" No priest can be so involved with hospital and patient without being forced to confront himself, and consequently this most important question must be asked. No matter how painful the process proves to be he must see himself as he really is. It may not be comfortable, but it will surely prove creative. All the feverish activity in the world will not help him reach his destination if all the while the fog of his own identity obscures the view. Why is he more eager "to do" than "to be"? He may see 500 patients a week yet be uninvolved and unaware of the deepest needs of any. Why is he happier with a nod or a smile six feet up rather than a down-to-earth confrontation with the patient or a senior member of staff?

In examining his function he must also be aware of what pastoral skills are needed in the exercise of his chaplaincy ministry. Practical issues will be discussed and demonstrated in groups and lecture-seminars, questions about the most effective methods of counselling and visiting, his sacramental ministry, his preaching, his worship, his own spiritual life (see Chapter 8).

The need to share with others some of one's own concerns will be paramount and there will be much opportunity given in a training programme for this to happen. When questionings, doubts, hopes, aspirations are honestly faced and openly talked through, such a ministry of sharing becomes a ministry of learning. The aim of such a training for chaplains will be seen

> not to make them into half-baked psychotherapists but to help them discover what they don't know and can't know, but nevertheless what they can know and how they can co-operate, and in the process help them to know themselves better, to accept themselves

more whole-heartedly, and so be able to give themselves in the strength of a newly found inner freedom.[1]

THE PROGRAMME

The structure of training programmes will naturally vary, but there are important and basic features which should be common to all:

1. *Ward visits.* Much of the student's time will be spent on wards, for here he will learn how to minister to people; here he will observe how they react to situations of fear, anxiety, and stress. Each participant in the programme will be assigned two or three wards in which he will learn to gain greater understanding of the dynamics of personality growth, to co-operate with all who are ministering to the patient, and to develop pastoral skills.

2. *Verbatim reports.* He will be expected to write up as fully and accurately as possible these pastoral interviews with patients. The reports will be worked out with both the supervisor and the other students. The writing and recalling of such pastoral visits will certainly prove an irksome exercise for the uninitiated, but they are of infinite value. They enable one, so to speak, to penetrate through the more superficial aspects of a pastoral call. The deeper meanings of a pastoral relationship become clearer and more defined and they serve as "a mirror of the student's emotional involvement with the patient". As a result of the reports each student will begin to understand the meaning of pastoral conversation and gain a further and deeper awareness of his feelings and failings in relationships with others, for real involvement is essential to a bedside ministry. It will not be his to diagnose—"Thou ailest here and here" (Goethe)—but to see the patient as a person in the light of him who heals and in whom there is no darkness at all. Not only will he come to understand the patient more

[1] *The Role of Religion in Mental Health* (N.A.M.H., 1967) p. 75.

9

meaningfully, but also himself more thoroughly.[1] No longer, will he be content to be "an-other", but will have "the courage to be" what he is—his *authentic self.*

SUPERVISION

The report will be discussed, either with the supervisor or in the group, and various points raised. Healthy and constructive criticism will arise as the working through of the report progresses stage by stage. Why did the student chaplain break off at a point when the patient was about to communicate her real feelings? Could questions have been framed more effectively to draw out more of the depression and anxiety the patient was obviously experiencing? Was there too much tendency to moralize or to sermonize? So the discussion will continue and a variety of factors be involved. All the time the question "Why?" will be asked as both chaplains and supervisor explore further concerns. Why does he have so much difficulty in presenting his written material? Why is he so eager to do things for the patient rather than be involved in a relationship? Accepting criticism in a healthy way without feeling threatened in the presence of others will be a learning process in itself and make for further growth and maturity. Alternative suggestions will always be offered for faulty responses: e.g., "Instead of saying what you did at that point, would it not have been more helpful to say . . .?" There will be few clear-cut right or wrong responses, but there will be some far more appropriate than others for each given situation. The personalities of supervisor and chaplains will also vary and play their part in the general discussions of a verbatim report, and each participant will learn from the success and failures of others.

Other important items in a training programme will be *lecture seminars*, *clinical conferences*, and *free discussion groups*, in which students can learn some of the dynamics of group work as well as insight into their own inner growth.

[1] For an outline of a typical verbatim report see Norman Autton, *The Pastoral Care of the Mentally Ill* (S.P.C.K., 1963) pp. 167–9.

There will be much *written work*, as well as *individual interviews*, for such supervision is a most essential part of the training programme. For this reason not more than five or six students should be allocated to each chaplain/supervisor.

A *final evaluation report* should be written by the student on what he has learned from his experience, his relationships with others and insights gained. It will also be the task of the supervisor to submit a concise and comprehensive report on the student's work and progress, commenting on his suitability to undertake hospital chaplaincy ministry.

Experiments are already taking place at various teaching hospitals in clinical training programmes for hospital chaplains, and it is to be hoped that in future no whole-time chaplain will be appointed unless he has undergone a significant period of supervised training in a recognized centre.[1] With such experience behind him he should be more adequately equipped for the responsibilities which will lie ahead in undertaking a chaplaincy ministry. He will have been given not only the necessary understanding and knowledge, as well as the acquisition of certain pastoral skills, but also a greater degree of confidence to take his place alongside other members of the hospital staff. In turn they will sense his ability and co-operation will be furthered.

[1] See Institute of Religion and Medicine, *Report on Consultation on Practical Training in Ministry*, I, 1966 and II, 1968; British Council of Churches, *Working Party on Theological Training*, 1968; and Hospital Chaplaincies Council, *Training Courses*.

8

The Chaplain himself

Ministering in hospital, where there is a continuous "giving out" and a continual contact with people, calls for some of the highest qualities of a priest. It is here, in the midst of the sufferings and anxieties of sick people, confronted daily with some of the most difficult, frustrating and discouraging situations in life, that the spiritual life of the chaplain is put to its most severe test. The following quotation comes from *The Bishoprick of Souls*, published in 1842, yet it has such an ageless message.

> In the sick chamber lies the test of the efficiency of your ministry. Seek it nowhere else; everywhere else the proof is confounded with the proof of mere adjuncts, which, however useful, may not be indispensable . . . but here you stand upon your character . . . yes, for the real work of the ministry you are quite incompetent, if you cannot stand by the sick man's bed a truly spiritual man.

Face to face with the basic issues of life and death he is forced either to remain aloof or to realize that he can only be adequate when he accepts his own inadequacy and becomes wholly dependent upon a power greater than himself.

To carry out his work effectively the chaplain will need to possess, in varying measure, the following seven qualities of character and temperament:

1. *He must be physically strong.* One of the dangers of the priesthood in the past was laziness; today it seems to be busyness. The ceaseless pressure of sheer numbers—staff, patients, families, etc. will make the hospital chaplain, part-time or whole-

time, particularly prone to such a danger. In his eagerness to cover the ground, in all senses of the term, his ministry can become superficial and external if it is not carefully watched; "As thy servant was busy here and there, he was gone" (1 Kings 21.41). "The clergyman's rule", states Monica Furlong, "must be to decrease his activity, to live much more in a state of being than doing. . . . To this one layman the clergy who help and impress most are those who live in a state which is neither laziness nor hyper-activity." [1] If the chaplain is to be an effective instrument in God's hands for his work of healing, then he must try and keep himself physically fit. It was St Teresa who wrote, "To pray well we must eat well and sleep well." The needs of Brother Body must be supplied. The chaplain's rule of life should be as strict about his hour of retirement as it is for his hour of rising. If he is overtired he can do no real visiting, for most of his work must be done on his feet. He will be frequently called out by night, and many an emergency will arise at rather inconvenient times, like the "sick-call" of Nicodemus to our Lord. The chaplain will be expected to respond, and his work to be cheerfully and contentedly done. Unless he has a disciplined rule of life his ministry will obviously lack order and lead to confusion.

Time is one of God's most precious gifts, and it is up to the chaplain to use it profitably and sensibly. His day-off-duty each week must be rigidly kept, as must be his outside interests and hobbies. This is particularly important for the chaplain whose whole time is spent in the hospital environment. "Six days thou shalt labour and do all thou hast to do." If he is to work the works of him who sent him efficiently and well then there will have to be a wise economy of energy, for "mastery is acquired by resolved limitations". If he attempts more than he should depression and frustration will soon catch up on him. Difficult as it so often is, he must learn to say, "I must accept what I cannot do or get done, or hinder, as soon as I have done all that is possible; then it is not negligence, but simple

[1] *Ourselves Your Servants* (A.C.C.M.) p. 26.

submissiveness to the Will of God."[1] St Vincent de Paul has something to say about the danger of overwork which every chaplain should heed:

> Have a care to keep your health for the love of our God and his poor members, and take care not to overdo yourself: it is the trick of the devil by which he deceives good souls, to entice them to do more than they can, so that they may be unable to do anything at all. The spirit of God on the contrary entices one gently to do good as reasonably as one can, so that one may do it perseveringly for a long time.[2]

2. *He must be socially adaptable.* "Let your light so shine before men that they may see. . ." Throughout his chaplaincy ministry the priest will meet a succession of strangers. There will be a constant "coming and going". Each day he will be making contact with new people, and he will be rightly expected to show his concern by sympathetic sharing and relating. It is therefore imperative that his whole personality be friendly, pleasing, and warm; honest rather than hearty, natural rather than affected. He should find it as easy to speak to the chairman in the boardroom as with the porter in the lodge, and nothing that interests them should fail to interest him. It was written of Forbes Robinson that

> here was one who compelled men, by his genuine unaffected interest in their lives and work, to be themselves genuinely interested in them too. A man could not know Forbes for long and not be quickly conscious of a new sense of the value of himself, which made him believe that his own personality and life were things of great importance. For "he is interested in me" is what almost every man felt from the start of his acquaintance with Forbes.[3]

If the chaplain can capture some of that "presence" then indeed will a hospital "see" and glorify the Father in heaven,

[1] J. H. R. Morrell, *The Heart of a Priest* (S.P.C.K., 1958) p. 67.

[2] Quoted in R. W. Evans, *The Bishoprick of Souls*, 1842.

[3] M. R. J. Manktelow, *Forbes Robinson: Disciple of Love* (S.P.C.K., 1961) pp. 12–13.

for each member will be led to say, "He saw in us all, however ordinary, however commonplace—yes, however unlovely were our lives—something, somewhere, of Jesus Christ."[1]

3. *He must be ecumenically flexible.* "Other sheep I have. . ." Throughout his ministry he will be meeting people of various denominations and of no creed at all. To each he will exercise charity and goodwill. All the various chaplains must work together, and it is as necessary for them to work as a team as for any other section of the hospital staff. Each will be ready to pass on to the others relevant information concerning patients or staff of their respective denominations. They will meet regularly together for prayer, discussion, and deliberations as to how best the whole chaplaincy ministry can be carried out in their hospital. Tolerance and understanding will be exercised as each will learn from the other for the common good of all they will serve. If such a spirit pervades the hospital then not only can the physical ills of mankind find healing but the spiritual ills which divide us may be healed as well.

4. *He must be emotionally mature.* In the constant struggle between emotional involvement and over-involvement each chaplain must find his own line of demarcation, difficult as this may be. There will be frequent demands on his sympathy, heavy burdens for him to bear, all exacting much emotional strain. He will need to be quiet when at times all about him is hustle and bustle; calm when others might be ruffled. Among his patients and staff there will be very varying temperaments, much prejudice to be broken down, and much moral courage needed.

Sick people are particularly sensitive to the moods of those who minister to them. If he is emotionally well adjusted, the chaplain will not look for praise or satisfaction to bolster up his own inadequacies, nor will he be one to probe for other people's problems to find answers to his own. He who is insecure will further his patients' insecurity; he who is fearful

[1] Ibid.

will increase others' fears; he who is tense will multiply tensions. If he is indecisive, those about him lose confidence. If he has no sense of humour those about him will be depressed. Not only will he need to say the right word at the right time but also be the right type of person to say it.

5. *He must be mentally alert.* ". . . and of a sound mind." There can be no "respectable inefficiency" in the mind of any hospital chaplain today when both science and theology are involved in so much new thinking. If he is not able to keep up his reading, stimulate his thinking, keep abreast of modern developments, his mind will soon become stagnant or just an empty pool. As well as one who is seen to move with certainty and conviction, he should be recognized as one who thinks constructively and clearly. If he has little to contribute when the obstetrician inquires about his views on abortion, when the houseman seeks advice on resuscitation, when the pharmacist is worried about drugs or clinical testing, or when the patient seeks advice on sterilization, then he has no right to be accepted as an essential member of the healing team, where every decision counts and competence is evident.

6. *He must be theologically sound.* The chaplain will be meeting some of the most baffling situations in life—a lingering painful death: the pain of a young child: a bereavement. Because he is what he is, he will be expected "to give an account of the faith that is in him". How can he possibly do this unless he himself is rooted and grounded in a strong religious faith and stands on an adequate theology? That agonizing question "Why?" will have to be answered, not with clichés or platitudes, but with frankness and honesty, and the chaplain must at least be strong and secure enough to face up to it. In his attempt to be all things to all men he will not sacrifice his theology, neither will he compromise divine truth.

7. *He must be spiritually alive.* "For their sakes I sanctify myself." There will be many occasions on which the chaplain will

be tempted to weaken his sense of vocation and respond to the popular cry of "Come down, O Man of God". But he must always visit as a priest or pastor. He cannot be in touch with other people until he is first in touch with God, which will involve the following five activities:

(a) *Praying to him:* "making mention of you in my prayers (Eph. 1.16; Rom. 1.9; 1 Thess. 1.2; Phil. 1.3; 2 Tim. 1.3; Philemon 4). His busy life must never interfere with his prayer life. The chaplain will be the "pray-er", the intercessor. The names at the end of so many of the Pauline epistles may mean very little to the modern reader, but what a wealth of individual and personal ministry they reveal. So the chaplain will offer the cares and concerns of his people one by one to our Lord—"John, Mary, . . . whom thou lovest is sick." Happy indeed is the chaplain who morning after morning has a few of his faithful in the hospital chapel with him to offer up the daily prayers of the Church, but "unhappy, indeed, is the priest who, because it is not so with him, fails to do for them what they will not do with him".[1] The chaplain's intercessions will have an effect not only upon his patients and others for whom he prays but also on himself. It was noticed of Ouranius in Law's *Serious Call* that as a result of his regular intercessory prayers "this devotion softens his heart, enlightens his mind, sweetens his temper, and makes everything that comes from him instructive, amiable, and affecting".

The very essence of the chaplain's work will be his constant intercession, for in its practice he will be giving expression to his love for his people and offering up the whole work of the hospital and its community. Sometimes it will be more important to speak to God about a patient than to speak to the patient about God. He will act as mediator for them to God and for God to them. Such

---

[1] J. Wareham, *The Priest and His People* (Mowbrays 1946) p. 145.

intercession will begin in penitence and end in thanks-giving. When faced with difficult tasks and problems which tax his strength, in his own private prayers he will recall those of Brother Lawrence: "I spoke hopefully to God that it was his business I was about, and then I found it very well performed".

(b) *Meditating upon him:* "Speak, Lord, for thy servant heareth" will be his sincere plea as in the silence of the early morning he takes his place in the chapel. While he thus muses the fire kindles, inflaming him with new energy, fresh courage, and renewed hope. What does God want of me today? It will be no breathless monologue, but a balance kept between silence and speech. When the busy world is hushed he will once again take advantage of that silence which Kierkegaard called "the homeliness of eternity".

(c) *Partaking of him:* At the altar all his ministry will find its fulfilment. He will offer up the hospital, its work, its people, and its very life. He will bring to the altar, for example, the work of the surgeon operating on the heart of a young child, and at that precise moment he becomes as vital a member of the theatre team as those who stand before another table where new life is being given and blood shed.

(d) *Learning from him:* The chaplain's bible reading, devotional reading, daily recitation of the divine office, annual retreat, and recourse to a spiritual director will be a constant strength and support, for there will be the need for frequent refreshment amid a ministry which entails so much "giving out". He will say the daily office not alone but on behalf of the whole Church in union with him who is its Head; the penitent on behalf of the impenitent, the pray-er on behalf of the prayerless; the thankful on behalf of the thankless; the believer on behalf of the unbeliever, and the forgiver on behalf of the unforgiving.

(e) *Companionship with him:* "Not I, but Christ liveth in me."
Patients will soon sense whether we ourselves have been
with Jesus.

> We do not need to speak much of Jesus [R. M. Benson once said],
> Jesus will speak from himself on our behalf. The natural heart can
> resist the most convincing arguments, but not the consuming fire of
> the divine life whereby we ought to be sanctified. If we live true to
> God, he will bring people to himself through us. It is not our work
> which brings them, it is his . . . We cannot bear witness to him,
> save by living in him. The more we are hidden from the world in
> him, the more will he use us as instruments for making himself
> known to the world. . . . Love makes a very small amount of
> matter go a long way. . . . People also take in, without knowing it,
> what comes to them as an atmosphere. . . . They are much more
> easily taught through the heart, in its wilderness, than through the
> head, in its regularity.[1]

If our very presence stamps us out as holy men of God, if we
bear about in us his very person, we shall be able to show to
our sick and afflicted people

> that eternal life, which was with the Father, and was manifested
> unto us; that which we have seen and heard declare we unto you,
> that ye also may have fellowship with us; and truly our fellowship
> is with the Father, and with his Son, Jesus Christ. . . . This then is
> the message we have heard of him, and declare unto you, that God
> is light, and in him is no darkness at all (1 John 1.2–5).

[1] *Thoughts from the Notebooks of a Priest Religious,* compiled by W. F.
Adams, S.S.J.E. (Faith Press, 1949) p. 15.

APPENDIX A

The National Health Service and the Chaplain

The National Health Service Act of 1946 required the Minister of Health "to promote the establishment in England and Wales of a comprehensive health service designed to secure improvement in the physical and mental health of the people of England and Wales and the prevention, diagnosis, and treatment of illness". In July 1948 the Hospital and Specialist Service (Part ii), the Local Health Authority Services (Part iii), and the Executive Council Service came into being. Some 2,600 hospitals with some half million beds in England and Wales are in the National Health Service, including the twenty-six teaching hospitals in London (with approximately a hundred hospitals, convalescent homes, branches, annexes, or treatment centres), and the ten provincial teaching hospitals (representing some seventy hospitals and other establishments).

REGIONAL HOSPITAL BOARDS

For purposes of administration the country was divided into fourteen Regional Hospital Boards in England and the Welsh Hospital Board, which are in general charge of the hospital and specialist services. They operate in areas associated with a university having a school of medicine. Each Regional Hospital Board has a membership of about twenty-two to thirty-two persons who are appointed in an honorary capacity by the Minister of Health in consultation with the universities, local health authorities, organizations representing the medical profession, voluntary associations, employers, and trade unions. Each member holds office for three years, one-third retiring annually and being eligible for re-appointment. The Regional Hospital Board is responsible *inter alia* for the carrying out of long-term development plans in its particular region, for the provision of special services, and the appointment of senior medical staff. The Regional Hospital

Boards do their work by means of various committees composed of members of the Board—General Purposes, Finance, Works and Buildings, Medical Services, etc.

BOARDS OF GOVERNORS OF TEACHING HOSPITALS

Hospitals are divided into two kinds for administrative purposes— teaching and non-teaching. The teaching hospital provides facilities for undergraduate and post-graduate clinical teaching. In England and Wales there are thirty-six, of which twenty-six (twelve under-graduate and post-graduate and fourteen post-graduate only) are situated in London. All teaching hospitals are administered by Boards of Governors which are responsible to the Minister alone for their organization and control. The members of the Boards are appointed by the Minister, three-fifths of them having been nominated in equal numbers by the university, the teaching staff, and the Regional Hospital Board for the area in which the hospital is situated.

HOSPITAL MANAGEMENT COMMITTEES

The 2,400 non-teaching hospitals under the Regional Hospital Boards are managed and controlled by some 350 Hospital Management Committees (with one exception, Wessex, each region has one or more teaching hospitals). The Hospital Management Committee is "to control and manage that hospital or group of hospitals on behalf of the Board, and for that purpose to exercise on behalf of the Board such of the functions of the Board relating to the hospital or group of hospitals as may be prescribed". The membership of the Management Committee is under the authority of the Regional Hospital Board in consultation with the local health authorities, the executive councils, the senior doctors and dentists working in the hospitals, and other interested bodies. The day-to-day running of the hospitals and their revenue expenditure and the appointment of all staff except senior medical and dental staff fall within their responsibility, and they have a considerable freedom of action, although they are subject to such regulation and direction as may be given by the Minister or the Boards.

ADMINISTRATIVE STAFF

The Noel Hall Report of 1957 divided the hospital administrative staff into three grades: (*a*) senior; (*b*) general administrative, and (*c*) junior administrative: with two additional grades for clerical officers: (*a*) general clerical and (*b*) separate groups for shorthand typists, machine operators, etc.

The Hospital Secretary or *Hospital Administrator* is the "business manager", in charge of the business side of the hospital. *The Group Secretary* is chief administrative officer of the hospitals which comprise a hospital group. He is often also Secretary of the principal hospital within that group.

The Treasurer, formerly known as *Finance Officer*, is in charge of the financial services, the preparation of estimates, the keeping of accounts, control of expenditure, the costing system, cash expenditure, and payment of wages.

The Supplies Officer is responsible for contracting of supplies, for their storage and distribution.

The Medical Records Officer maintains the statistics of admissions and discharges, etc. In co-operation with the medical staff he is responsible for the design and handling of all medical records.

There are also officers in charge of other services.

The Catering Officer is responsible for ordering of supplies for the catering department, budgeting and cost control. The catering officer runs the kitchen, the preparation of meals and menus, and their distribution and service.

The Dietician advises the Catering Officer on dietetic matters and nutritive quality of menus. She supervises the preparation of diet sheets and their observance. Her most important work is carried out in the diabetic and metabolic clinics or units.

The Domestic Supervisor sees to the management of the housekeeping staff and is responsible for the training of new staff, their allocation of duties, and supervision. The Supervisor is to maintain proper standards of cleanliness and the efficiency of routine cleaning throughout the hospital.

The Laundry Superintendent is in charge of the hospital laundry. More and more hospitals are now concentrating laundry work on central hospital laundries.

The Building Supervisor is in charge of building maintenance and has the supervision of bricklayers, painters, joiners, plasterers, etc.

The Engineer is in charge of engineering, electrical, and plumbing services in the hospital or group. He also has supervision of sterilizers and ventilating plants.

The Pharmacist controls the supply and issue of drugs. He consults with medical staff on cost and pharmaceutical quality of various drugs.

MEDICAL STAFF

In hospitals throughout the country there are at present eight grades of medical staff. (See Royal Commission on Medical Education 1965–68: Cmmd 3569: *Report*: H.M.S.O. April 1968.)

The Consultant is at the top of the clinical hierarchy. (In the National Health Service there are twenty-one different consultant categories: general medicine; diseases of chest; mental health, neurology; paediatrics, radiology; radiotherapy; physical medicine, pathology; infectious diseases; gynaecology and obstetrics; dermatology; venereal diseases; ophthalmology; general surgery; anaesthetics; neurosurgery; plastic surgery; thoracic surgery; traumatic and orthopaedic surgery; ear, nose, and throat surgery.)

A consultant's post is normally obtained between the ages of 32–40 after having successfully acquired the necessary qualifications. The consultant has the oversight of the other grades.

The Senior Hospital Medical Officer. (If the recommendations of the Platt Report are taken up this grade will be replaced by the *Assistant Medical Officer.*)

The Senior Registrar, who is training to be a consultant and who would normally hold this post for some three to six years before attaining to consultant rank.

The Junior Hospital Medical Officer, whose rank like that of his senior equivalent will probably become obsolete.

The Registrar, who holds this rank normally for two years.

The Senior House Officer, the *House Officer*, and finally the *Pre-Registration House Officer*, which is the compulsory year of internship after qualification but prior to full admission to the medical register.

The first three grades are appointed by the Regional Hospital Board; the remainder by the Hospital Management Committees or Committee.

The Medical Student qualifies after six years' study and passes the final examination of a licensing Body or the Faculty of Medicine of a university. Then he obtains degrees such as M.B., B.S. (London), or diplomas such as M.R.C.S. (Eng.); L.R.C.P. (London).

NURSING STAFF

The most senior posts are *Matron, Deputy Matron, Assistant Matron*, and *Departmental* and *Ward Sisters*. In addition, in many hospitals there is a nurses' training school with its *Principal Tutor* and *Sister Tutors*. First, second, and third year nurses are known as *Student Nurses* and have to satisfy certain educational requirements of the General Nursing Council. Some hospitals, particularly the teaching hospitals, with a lengthy waiting-list of applicants, can demand a higher standard. Student nurses can be trained only at approved schools of nursing, and commence at 18 years of age. The Introductory Course in the Preliminary Training School lasts for eight weeks before the student begins her official nursing duties on the wards. After three years her training is completed and she qualifies as an S.R.N. (State Registered Nurse) R.M.N. (Registered Mental Nurse), or R.S.C.N. (Registered Sick Children's Nurse). For R.F.N. (Registered Fever Nurse) the training is only two years.

State Enrolled Nurses have a course of training which is primarily practical, and during which time they are known as pupil nurses. After one year there is an assessment test and after the second year as a senior pupil the nurse is enrolled.

Nursing Cadets are young boys and girls of 16 who are being trained in cadet schemes which are run in some hospitals. Normally they spend one or two full days a week at a college for further education. Their maximum working hours in both college and hospital are forty a week. They usually spend three months at a time in various departments of the hospital and do not become attached to hospital wards until they are 17.

Nursing Assistants are usually untrained personnel who work part-time. In the psychiatric hospital they are normally known as *Nursing Auxiliaries*. Recently short courses of instruction have been arranged for them.[1]

MEDICAL SOCIAL WORKERS

The duty of the Medical Social Worker is "to supplement the work of the doctor by adding social information to assist in the doctor's diagnosis and treatment, and to work with the patient and his family to minimize personal anxieties and to arrange for co-operation with other social services including those of the local authority".[2] Stress is laid upon casework, which is described in the Younghusband Report (p. 182) as "a personal service provided by qualified workers for individuals who require skilled assistance in resolving some material, emotional, or character problem".

PSYCHIATRIC SOCIAL WORKERS

A caseworker with an effective understanding of psychology and psychiatric problems is occupied with mental, maladjusted or other cases in attempts to discover their difficulties. The psychiatric social worker, like the medical social worker, is able to supply the medical authorities with a social case history of the patient, and serves as an important link between the psychiatric hospital and the community.

MENTAL WELFARE OFFICERS

Formerly referred to as "Duly Authorized Officers", Mental Welfare Officers are "local authority staff with duties of assisting in the legal aspects of the procedure for compulsory removal to hospital and of arranging the actual removal of patients".[3]

---

[1] For the future pattern of nursing administration see *Structure According to Salmon*, Report of the Committee on Senior Nursing Staff Structure. Reprinted from the *Nursing Times*, 13 May 1966, and available from Macmillan & Co., Brunel Road, Basingstoke, Hants, price 1s.

[2] Peters and Kinnaird, *Health Services Administration* (Livingstone, 1965) pp. 262–3.

[3] Ibid., p. 284.

10

A HOSPITAL PLAN
FOR ENGLAND AND WALES

This was a White Paper published by H.M.S.O. in 1962, and was the first comprehensive rebuilding plan. It lists 90 new and 134 remodelled hospitals to be commenced by 1970–71. The Plan is to be revised each year. One of its important developments is the comprehensive district general hospital of 600–800 beds serving a population of 100,000–150,000. This will mean the closure of many of the smaller hospitals, bringing all the various branches of medicine under one roof. They will contain all the in-patient and out-patient facilities as well as units for maternity work, psychiatry, geriatrics, and infectious diseases.

THE HOSPITAL CHAPLAINCY SERVICE

When the National Health Service was set up it was stated by the Government that the State should provide chaplains for all those in its care in hospitals. The Ministry of Health has issued two comprehensive memoranda: *Appointment of Hospital Chaplains* (HM(63)80) and *Remuneration and Conditions of Service of Hospital Chaplains* (HM (63)81) to all Hospital Management Committees and to the Boards of Governors of Teaching hospitals relating to the hospital chaplaincy service. It is essential that every chaplain should have a copy of these and take note of their important contents. The circular HM(63)80 states that

> in all hospitals, Hospital Management Committees and Boards of Governors should give special attention to providing for the spiritual needs of patients and staff and, in particular, should do everything possible so to arrange the hours of duty as to enable staff and students to attend the services etc. of their own denomination.

APPOINTMENT OF CHAPLAINS

The same circular recommends (para. 3) that

> the Committees or Board should appoint a whole-time or part-time chaplain—or chaplains from more than one denomination—for every hospital for which they are responsible, and these appointments should always be made in consultation with the appropriate

Church authorities. For Anglican appointments the Regional Hospital Board should, in conjunction with the Boards of Governors of the teaching hospitals in their area, themselves set up an advisory committee for the purpose, after consulting the bishops of the dioceses concerned. Roman Catholic appointments should be made in consultation with the bishop of the Roman Catholic diocese in which the hospital lies. Free Church appointments should be made in consultation with the National Free Church Federal Council (27 Tavistock Square, London, W.C.1). For whole-time Anglican and Free Church appointments it is suggested that the Regional chaplaincies advisory committee or the National Free Church Federal Council, as appropriate, should be invited to put forward names of candidates they regard as suitable and to comment on any other candidates.

Circular HM(63)80 also states (para. 4):

The appointment of whole-time hospital chaplains should not be for an indefinite period and the Minister suggests to Hospital Management Committees and Boards of Governors that appointments of Anglican and Free Church chaplains should be made for a period of five years in the first instance (subject to the provisions of paragraph 5 below), the appointment then being capable of renewal, in consultation with the Regional chaplaincies advisory committee or the National Free Church Federal Council, for a further five years, and exceptionally for further periods; the period of appointment of Roman Catholic chaplains should be determined in consultation with the bishop of the Roman Catholic diocese.

It is the decision of each Hospital Management Committee or Board of Governors whether a whole-time or part-time chaplain is appointed. Para. 6 suggests that

In some cases it may be convenient to have one whole-time chaplain to serve the patients and staff of a particular denomination in all the hospitals in the group; in others the service may be more conveniently provided by one or more part-time chaplains. The appointment of whole-time chaplains may be made where there are 750 patients or more of one denomination, no account being taken of the number of staff who minister in the respective hospital.

If a hospital has had a whole-time chaplain in the past and is "not substantially smaller" then "this practice may be continued". A part-time chaplain should not be required to serve more than 300 patients and "where the average number of patients calculated on the average for the preceding three years exceeds 300, more than one part-time appointment should be made". It is hoped that Hospital Management Committees and Boards will ensure that a sufficiently lengthy period of notice is given when a chaplaincy appointment is terminated, as directed in H.M. (68) 18.

In order that there might be a clear mutual understanding of the nature of the obligation involved in a part-time chaplaincy appointment a notional session scale was compiled as follows:

NUMBER OF PATIENTS	NUMBER OF SESSIONS (of 3½ hrs)
6–25	½
26–50	1
51–80	1½
81–120	2
121–160	2½
161–200	3
201–250	3½
251–300	4

It is essential for a newly-appointed chaplain to receive a letter of appointment from the Hospital Management Committee or Board, and it is equally important that upon resignation of his office due notification of termination of appointment be given by the chaplain.

Whole-time chaplains are licensed by the Bishop concerned, and part-time chaplains should also be specifically licensed as such if the hospitals in which they minister are not situated within the boundaries of their respective parishes. It is extremely helpful to the chaplain if the licensing is performed publicly in the hospital chapel.

Whole-time chaplaincies are pensionable under the Health Service Superannuation Scheme unless the 1948 Clergy Pensions Measure applies to them. The Pensions Board makes it clear that a hospital chaplaincy is an ecclesiastical officer and not a public post. Under Ministry of National Insurance regulations a whole-time chaplain is deemed to be an employed person for the purposes of National Insurance.

All chaplains are entitled to claim travelling expenses on the same basis as other officials of the hospital staff in respect of journeys from one hospital to another in the course of duty, but not from home to the hospital apart from emergencies to which they might be called.

HOSPITAL CHURCH SISTERS

At the time of writing there are twelve hospital church sisters in England, and the Ministry of Health are prepared to sanction their remuneration from Exchequer funds, provided they are satisfied that the appointment is necessary to supplement the work of the chaplains. The church sister is not a secretarial assistant to the chaplain, nor a substitute for the priest; rather does her ministry complement that of the chaplain, sharing with him a pastoral relationship on an equal basis towards the whole hospital and its community.

NOTE: For the work of the Church Assembly Hospital Chaplaincies Council and its Joint Committee (comprising representatives of the Free Church Federal Council and the Roman Catholic Church), the Church of England Hospital Chaplains' Fellowship, and the National Association of Whole-time Hospital Chaplains, see *A King's Fund Report: The Hospital Chaplain, an Enquiry into the Role of the Hospital Chaplain* (Published by King Edward's Hospital Fund, 1966).

APPENDIX B

Common Medical and Surgical Abbreviations

COMMON MEDICAL AND SURGICAL ABBREVIATIONS

B.I.D.	Brought in dead
C.A.	Carcinoma
D.I.	Dangerously ill
D.O.A.	Dead on arrival
D.S.	Disseminated sclerosis
D.U.	Duodenal ulcer
E.C.G.	Electro-cardiogram
E.C.T.	Electro-convulsive therapy
E.E.G.	Electro-encephalogram
E.N.T.	Ear, nose and throat
Inf.	Infirmary
I.T.	Industrial therapy
I.Q.	Intelligence quotient
L.A.	Local anaesthetic
M.S.	Mentally subnormal
M.S.W.	Medical social worker
M.W.O.	Mental welfare officer
N.A.	No anaesthetic
O.T.	Occupational therapy
P.R.	*Per rectum* (examination)
P.V.	*Per vagina* (examination)
R.M.O.	Resident medical officer
S.H.M.O.	Senior hospital medical officer
S.I.	Seriously ill
S./N.	Staff nurse
T.B.	Tuberculosis
V.D.	Venereal disease

-ectomy	cutting out, removal
-itis	inflammation
-ology	study of
-ostomy	outlet
-otomy	opening
-scopy	see into, examine
-sclerosis	hardening
-stenosis	narrowing of opening

APPENDIX C

A Selection of Useful Literature for Distribution to Patients

Daily Prayer Ed. E. Milner-White and G. W. Briggs (Pelican 1961).

Daily Prayer and Praise George Appleton (World Christian Books 1966).

One Man's Prayers George Appleton (S.P.C.K. 1967).

Acts of Devotion George Appleton (S.P.C.K. 1963).

A Hospital Prayer Book (O.U.P. 1966).

My Day with Jesus: Prayers and Acts for Private Use (Mirfield publication).

Light in the Night A Religious of C.S.M.V. (S.C.M.).

A Pocket Book for Christians A Religious of C.S.M.V. (S.C.M.).

Prayers on the Sermon on the Mount Margaret Cropper (S.C.M.).

A Form of Thanksgiving to Almighty God after a Serious Illness (S.P.C.K.).

Private Devotions Compiled by Presbyter Anglicanus (S.P.C.K. 1959).

Prayers for Patients Ed. A. Kellett (Arthur James Ltd. 1964).

Personal Consecration: A Short Litany for Private Use (Mowbrays).

St Raphael Book of Prayers for the Sick (S.P.C.K. 1963).

St Raphael Book of Prayers for the Use of The Sick (S.P.C.K.).

Our Response to God: Far and Near (Forward Movement Publications: Bi-monthly booklet of intercession).

When You Are Ill B. T. Guy (S.P.C.K.).

A Little Book about Holy Unction Purcell Fox (Guild of St Raphael publication).

Ten Days in Hospital G. Lovell (Epworth Press).

For Your Comfort: A Booklet for the Use of Patients in Hospital (Churches' Council of Healing).

Toward the Light (Hospital Chaplaincy Department, Free Church Federal Council).

Beginning with You and Ending with God (Hospital Chaplaincy Department, Free Church Federal Council).

Prayers for Use in Sickness (Church Union).

Card to send to Sick People (Guild of St Raphael).

Holy Communion Thoughts for the Sick (Guild of St Raphael).

Bedside Prayer Cards for the Sick (S.P.C.K.).

A Simple Talk to Those who are Ill Lindsay Dewar (Guild of St Raphael

The Church's Help in Sickness T. W. Crafer (Guild of St Raphael).

Some Bible Sentences for Your Prayers and Meditations (Guild of Health).

A Message of Hope for the Sick J. Wilson (Guild of Health).

In Face of Fear A Religious of C.S.M.V. (S.P.C.K.).

The Conquest of Fear H. C. Robins (S.P.C.K.).

Going into Hospital D. G. Jones (S.P.C.K. Christian Knowledge Booklet, 1965).

Creative Suffering Julia de Beausobre (Dacre Press).

For Those Who are Ill H. W. Charity (Epworth Press).

Why Me? F. Barrie Flint (Mothers' Union).

In Sickness K. N. Ross (S.P.C.K.).

The Christian Hope (S.P.C.K. 3240: on card 3240A).

Pater Noster: A Meditation on the Lord's Prayer (S.P.C.K. 1960).

PACTS: A Pattern for Prayer (Mirfield publication).

Think of Our Lord Speaking to You (Mirfield publication).

Facing Pain—Hamilton King's Sermon in the Hospital (Mirfield publication).

To Help You Pray Hugh Montefiore (S.P.C.K. Christian Knowledge Booklet).

Practice of the Presence of God Brother Lawrence (Mowbrays).

Baptism (The Country Churchman, No. 1).

Upbringing (The Country Churchman, No. 5).

The Gospels (in booklet form) (British and Foreign Bible Society).

In His Presence (Mothers' Union).

APPENDIX D

Various Organizations
relevant to Chaplains' Work[1]

The Church Assembly Hospital Chaplaincies Council: Church House, Dean's Yard, Westminster, S.W.1.

The Hospital Chaplains' Fellowship (Secretary elected annually), c/o The Hospital Chaplaincies Council (above).

The Free Church Hospital Chaplains' Fellowship: Hospital Chaplaincy Board, Free Church Federal Council, 27 Tavistock Square, London, W.C.1.

National Association of Whole-time Hospital Chaplains (Interdenominational): The Rev. Ronald Stevenson, Lancaster Moor Hospital, Lancaster.

National Association for Mental Health: 39 Queen Anne Street, London, W.1.

Association of Hospital Matrons: 17 Portland Place, London, W.1.

King Edward's Hospital Fund: 14 Palace Court, Bayswater, London, W.2.

Churches' Council of Healing: 16 Lincoln's Inn Fields, London, W.C.2.

Institute of Religion and Medicine: 58A Wimpole Street, London, W.1.

London Medical Group (Institute of Religion and Medicine) 103 Gower Street, London, W.C.1.

Guild of St Raphael, 77 Kinnerton Street, London, S.W.1.

Guild of Health: 26 Queen Anne Street, London, W.1.

Divine Healing Mission: The Old Rectory, Crowhurst, Nr. Battle, Sussex.

The Dorothy Kerin Home of Healing; Burrswood, Groombridge, Nr Tunbridge Wells, Kent.

Union of St Luke for Doctors and Clergy: 106 Frithville Gardens, London, W.12.

Guild of Pastoral Psychology: 41 Redcliffe Gardens, London, S.W.10.

The Inter-Hospital Nurses' Christian Fellowship: 35 Catherine Street, London, S.W.1.

The Nurses' Fellowship within the Mothers' Union: Mary Sumner House, Tufton Street; London, S.W.1.

The Guild of St Barnabas for Anglican Nurses. 17 Portland Place, London, W.1.

Catholic Nurses' Guild of England and Wales: Bevendean Hospital, Brighton 7, Sussex.

The Discovery Foundation for Christian work among Nurses and Associated Professions, 4 Eastern Road, Selly Park, Birmingham 29.

Clinical Theology Association: "Lingdale", Weston Avenue, Mount Hooton Road, Nottingham.

The Richmond Fellowship: 8 Addison Road, Kensington, W.14.

Diploma in Pastoral Studies: Department of Theology, University of Birmingham 15.

Diploma of Pastoral Studies: New College, The Mound, Edinburgh 1.

Diploma in Pastoral Studies: University College, Cardiff.

---

[1] For up to date addresses and telephone numbers of these and similar organizations, see *The Church of England Year Book*, C.I.O. published annually.

Bibliography

CHAPTER 1

The Hospital Chaplain in *Contact*, No. 16 (January 1966).

The Hospital Ministry, by Norman Autton (Church's Ministry Series, No. 6, C.I.O., 1966).

The Church is Healing, by Michael Wilson (S.C.M. Press, 1966).

Ordeal of Wonder, by E. R. Morgan (O.U.P., 1964).

Christian Faith and Pastoral Care, by C. D. Keane (S.P.C.K., 1961).

The Hospital Chaplain. A King's Fund Report. (Publ. King Edward's Hospital Fund, 1966).

A Guide for Spiritual Directors, by the Author of *The Way* (Mowbrays).

The Healing Church. Report: Tübingen Consultation (W.C.C., 1965).

Evil and the God of Love, by J. Hick (Macmillan, 1967).

Community, Religion and Healing, by R. A. Lambourne (Darton, Longman & Todd, 1963).

People in Hospital, by E. Barnes (Macmillan, 1961).

Liturgy and Worship, edited by W. K. Lowther Clarke (S.P.C.K., 1933), pp. 472–615.

Pastoral Care in a Changing World, by Erastus Evans (Epworth Press, 1961).

CHAPTER 2

Sick Call, by Kenneth Child (S.P.C.K. Library of Pastoral Care, 1965).

Caring for the Elderly, by H. P. Steer (S.P.C.K. Library of Pastoral Care, 1966).

The Pastoral Care of the Dying, by Norman Autton (S.P.C.K. Library of Pastoral Care, 1966).

The Pastoral Care of the Bereaved, by Norman Autton (S.P.C.K. Library of Pastoral Care, 1967).

A Grief Observed, by C. S. Lewis (Faber & Faber, 1961).

Care of the Dying, by C. Saunders (*Nursing Times* Reprint: Macmillan, 1959).

Dying, by John Hinton (Pelican Original, 1967).

Pain and Providence, by L. Boros (Burns & Oates, 1966).

The Moment of Truth, by L. Boros (Burns & Oates, 1965).

Triumph over Fear, by D. M. Wilson (Gollancz, 1966).

Human Behaviour in Illness, by L. Gillis (Faber & Faber, 1962).

The Problem of Pain, by C. S. Lewis (Fontana, 1957).

Man's Pain and God's Goodness, by J. V. Langmead Casserley (Mowbrays, 1951).

A Parson's Thoughts on Pain, by G. E. Childs (Mowbrays, 1949).

Le Milieu Divin, by Teilhard de Chardin (Collins, 1960).

Hospitals of the Long-Stay Patient, by D. Norton (Pergamon Press, 1967).

CHAPTER 3

Psychology, the Nurse and the Patient, by D. Odlum (Nursing Mirror, 3rd edn, 1959).

Doctors and Patients, by Mark Hodson (Hodder & Stoughton, 1967).

The Patients' Attitude to Nursing Care, by A. McGhie (Livingstone, O.P.).

Decisions About Life and Death. Report: Church Assembly Board for Social Responsibility (C.I.O., 1965).

Abortion. Report: Church Assembly Board for Social Responsibility (C.I.O., 1965).

Some Moral Problems, by T. Wood (S.P.C.K. Seraph, 1965).

Nurse and Patient Relationship, by Genevieve Burton (Tavistock publications, 1965).

To the Anglican Nurse (C.I.O., revised, 1967).

Christianity and Nursing Today. Report: Nurses Christian Movement (1963/64).

Ethical Responsibility in Medicine, by V. Edmunds and C. G. Scorer (E. & S. Livingstone, 1967).

Moral Responsibility in Clinical Research, by D. McG. Jackson (Tyndale Press, 1958).

The Christian Nurse, by M. Wilson (Edinburgh House Press, 1960).

Clergy-Doctor Co-operation (C.I.O., 1963).

Ethics and Medical Practice, by J. Marshall (Darton, Longman & Todd, 1960).

Co-operation: Doctors and Patients: Priest and People (Guild of St Raphael, 1957).

CHAPTER 5

The Administration of the Sacraments in Hospital, by Malcolm Osborne (Mowbrays, 1961).
Holy Unction: A Practical Guide to its Administration, by Henry Cooper (Guild of St Raphael, July 1966; revised edition).
The Church's Ministry of Healing. Report of Archbishops' Commission (C.I.O., 1958).
The Church's Ministry of Healing, by A. H. P. Fox (Longmans, 1959).
I was Sick and Ye Visited Me, by M. M. Martin (Faith Press, 1958).
The Priest's Vade Mecum, edited by T. W. Crafer (S.P.C.K., 1945).
The Anointing of the Sick by F. W. Puller, s.s.J.E. (S.P.C.K., 1910).
Comfort and Sure Confidence, by A. W. Hopkinson (Mowbray, 1927).
The Administration of Holy Unction and the Laying on of Hands. Convocation of Canterbury and Convocation of York (S.P.C.K., 1936).
The Healing Church, by W. J. T. Kimber (S.P.C.K., 1962).

CHAPTER 6

Psychiatry and the Christian Faith, by J. Dominian (Burns & Oates, 1962).
Healing the Sick Mind, by H. Guntrip (Unwin Books, 1964).
Psychiatry Today, by D. Stafford Clark (Pelican, 1952).
What Freud Really Said, by D. Stafford Clark (Pelican, 1967).
Introduction to Psychotherapy, by J. A. Hadfield (Allen & Unwin, 1967).
New Horizons in Psychiatry, by P. Hays (Pelican, 1964).
Group Psychotherapy, by S. H. Foulkes & E. J. Anthony (Pelican, 1957).
The Pastoral Care of the Mentally Ill, by Norman Autton (S.P.C.K., 1963).
Disorders of the Emotional and Spiritual Life, by W. L. Northridge (Epworth, 1960).
Adventure in Psychiatry, by D. V. Martin (Bruno Cassirer, 1962).
Religion and Mental Health. Report: National Association for Mental Health (1960).
Freud and Christianity, by R. S. Lee (Clarke, 1949; reprinted as a Pelican book, 1967).
Psychiatry for Students, by D. Stafford Clark (Allen & Unwin, 1964).

An Approach to Community Mental Health, by G. Caplan (Tavistock, 1961).
Everybody's Business; The Mental Health Act and The Community, by Nesta Roberts (N.A.M.H., 1960).
Beyond all Reason, by Moray Coate (Constable, 1964).
Mental Illness and Social Work, by Eugene Heimler (Pelican Original, 1967).
The Psychotic, by Andrew Crowcroft (Pelican Original, 1967).
Number Unknown. Report of Children's Council Working Party (C.I.O., 1965).

CHAPTER 7

The Pastor as Counsellor, by André Godin (Logos Books, Gill & Son, 1965).
The Faith of the Counsellors, by P. Halmos (Constable, 1965).
The Casework Relationship, by Felix Biestek (S.C.M. Press, 1961).
Casework and Pastoral Care, by Joan Heywood (S.P.C.K. Library of Pastoral Care, 1967).
An Introduction to Teaching Casework Skills, by J. Heywood (Routledge & Kegan Paul, 1964).
Biology and Personality, edited by I. T. Ramsey (Blackwell, 1965).
The Compassionate Society, by K. Jones (S.P.C.K. Seraph, 1967).
The Meaning of Persons, by P. Tournier (S.C.M. Press, 1957).
Christians and Social Work, by K. Heasman (S.C.M. Press, 1965).
Healing through Counselling, by H. W. Kyle (Epworth Press, 1964).
The Nature of the Pastoral Ministry, by E. James (Prism Pamphlet No. 32).
Clergy Training Today, by Basil Moss (S.P.C.K., 1964).
Learning to be Human. Report: British Council of Churches, 1968.
The Doctor, the Patient and his Illness, by M. Balint (Pitman, 1957).
Human Growth and the Development of Personality, by J. H. Kahn (Pergamon Press, 1965).

CHAPTER 8

Psychology and the Parish Priest, by Lindsay Dewar (Mowbrays, O.P.).
Modern Man: The Spiritual Life, by M. Thurian (Lutterworth Press, O.P.).
Forbes Robinson: Disciple of Love, by M. R. J. Manktelow (S.P.C.K., 1961).

Christian Priesthood, by H. Balmforth (S.P.C.K., 1963).

The Christian Response, by Michel Quoist (Logos Books, Gill & Son, 1965).

Ourselves Your Servants (A.C.C.M., 1967).

A Priest's Notebook of Prayer, by J. H. L. Morrell (S.P.C.K., 1968).

The Heart of a Priest, by J. H. L. Morrell (S.P.C.K., 1962).

The Prayers of the New Testament, by F. D. Coggan (Hodder & Stoughton, 1967).

The Whole Person in a Broken World, by P. Tournier (Collins, 1965).

Life and Letters of R. Somerset Ward, edited by G. R. Morgan (Mowbrays, 1963).

Spirituality for Today, edited by Eric James (S.C.M. Press, 1968).

APPENDIX A

Health Services in Britain. Central Office of Information Reference Pamphlet 20 (H.M.S.O., 1964).

The Doctor and his World, by J. G. Thwaites (Gollancz, 1964).

Health Services Administration, by R. J. Peters and J. Kinnaird (E. & S. Livingstone, 1965).

Standards for Morale: Cause and Effect in Hospitals. Report by R. W. Revans (O.U.P., 1964).

Guide to the Social Services (Family Welfare Association).

The Shape of Hospital Management in 1980? (King Edward's Hospital Fund, 14 Palace Court, London, W.2., 1967).

Communication between Doctors, Nurses and Patients: an aspect of Human Relations in the Hospital Service (H.M.S.O., 1963).

The Pattern of the In-Patient's Day (H.M.S.O., 1961).

The Reception and Welfare of In-Patients in Hospital (H.M.S.O., 1953).

The Evolution of Hospitals in Britain (Pitman Medical Publications, 1964).

Human Relations and Hospital Care, by Ann Cartwright (Routledge & Kegan Paul, 1964).

Information Booklets for Guidance to Patients (King Edward's Hospital Fund, 14 Palace Court, London, W.2., 1962).

Hospital Internal Communications (King Edward's Hospital Fund, British Hospital Journal and Social Science Review, August 1965).

Index